QUICK&EASY
STITCHED JEWELRY

DEDICATION
My thanks to the unfailing support and patience of my family and friends and the creative minds and hearts of the Kalmbach Books Department.

Kalmbach Books
21027 Crossroads Circle
Waukesha, Wisconsin 53186
www.JewelryAndBeadingStore.com

Published in 2016
20 19 18 17 16   1 2 3 4 5

Manufactured in China

ISBN: 978-1-62700-231-8
EISBN: 978-1-62700-232-5

Editor: Erica Swanson
Book Design: Carole Ross
Photographer: William Zuback

Library of Congress Control Number: 2015941328

QUICK&EASY
STITCHED JEWELRY

**CATHY
JAKICIC**

Waukesha, Wisconsin

CONTENTS

Introduction 6

Projects

Beader's dozen *necklace & earrings* 10

Lush loops *necklace & bracelet* 15

Circular logic *necklace & earrings* 19

p.19

Grasping at (colorful) straws
necklace & bracelet 23

Twin spins *pendant, earrings, & bracelet* 28

Painting with beads *bracelet* 33

Style in the round *necklace & bracelet* 38

Raising the bar *necklaces* 42

Stitch up a banner day *necklace* 48

Delicate details *necklace* 52

Front & center *necklace* 56

p.31

Bicone bands *necklaces*..................... 60

Tiny tapestries *bracelet & necklace* 65

A stylish, tile-ish look *bracelet* 70

Ombre reef *necklace & earrings* 74

Beaded greenery *necklace*.................. 78

It's OK to bail *necklace & earrings* 83

Triangle trios *necklaces* 88

Herringbone flair *necklace* 92

St. Petersburg Square *necklaces* 96

Basics

Basic Techniques................................... 102

Tools and Materials............................. 107

About the Author 111

p.59

p.10

p.77

INTRODUCTION

My idea of heaven? A beading class every day, endless time to bead, and a world of art shows and online sites at which I can share and sell my work for a price that represents the time and skill it takes to create stitched and woven jewelry. There are also margaritas involved and I'm wearing yoga pants all the time.

You're on your own with the cocktails and clothes, but this book tries to bring a little heaven down to earth on other scores. I created these projects for both the new stitcher who wants to dip a toe in without committing to a 40-hour necklace, and the more experienced beader who's looking for project ideas for an afternoon, evening, or a rare lazy weekend. Also, for those of you who sell stitched jewelry and want something to tag with a lower price point that reflects the quick turnaround—here are some great ideas.

And while I would never support teaching or selling someone else's designs without their permission—everything in this book is yours. I don't sell my jewelry or teach very often, so you're not threatening my livelihood. These designs were designed for sharing. Enjoy!

A FEW PRACTICAL NOTES

The necklace lengths are measured without pendants. I included the exact colors and sources whenever possible, but many things came from my stash, so I offered educated guesses on the colors whenever possible.

Also, I know you're not going to read the book cover to cover, but I'd recommend browsing through all of the tips. There is a lot of information that would be helpful for a number of projects. I post many tips on my Facebook site, too. Join the fun at www.facebook.com/BeadingInsider.

PROJECTS

Beader's dozen

I was introduced to these twelve-bead wonders in a bead class. This simple beaded sphere is the most basic of geometric beaded beads. Over the years, I've added my own ideas and experimented with different effects that specific color arrangements can make.

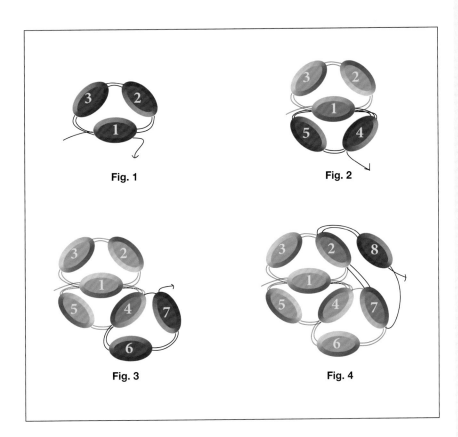

Fig. 1

Fig. 2

Fig. 3

Fig. 4

Beaded bead

1. Condition a 24-in. (61cm) piece of beading thread (Basics, p. 104) and thread a needle on one end. Pick up three pinch beads (1, 2, and 3), and tie an overhand knot (Basics, p. 104), leaving a 2-in. (5cm) tail. Sew back through beads 1, 2, 3, and 1. Pull the thread tight after every step **(fig. 1)**.

2. Pick up beads 4 and 5. Sew through 1, 4, 5, 1, and 4 **(fig. 2)**.

3. Pick up beads 6 and 7. Sew through beads 4, 6, and 7 **(fig. 3)**.

4. Sew back through bead 2. Pick up bead 8, and sew through beads 7, 2, and 8 **(fig. 4)**.

Supplies

Beaded bead

- **12** 5x3mm pinch beads
- Beading thread
- Beading needles, #10–#12
- Thread conditioner
- Scissors

Chain necklace, 20 in. (51cm)

- **3** beaded beads
- **6** 4mm round beads
- **3** 5x3mm pinch beads
- 22 in. (56cm) cable chain, 4mm links
- Flexible beading wire, .014
- **2** or **3** 10mm jump rings
- **3** 2-in. (5cm) headpins
- Lobster-claw clasp
- Roundnose pliers and chainnose pliers
- Diagonal wire cutters

Earrings

- **2** beaded beads
- **4** 4mm round beads
- **2** 5x3mm pinch beads
- **4** links cable chain, 4mm links
- **2** 2-in. (5cm) headpins
- Pair of earring wires
- Roundnose and chainnose pliers
- Diagonal wire cutters

Color Guide
Pearls: petrol
Pinch beads: gold, turquoise, and red

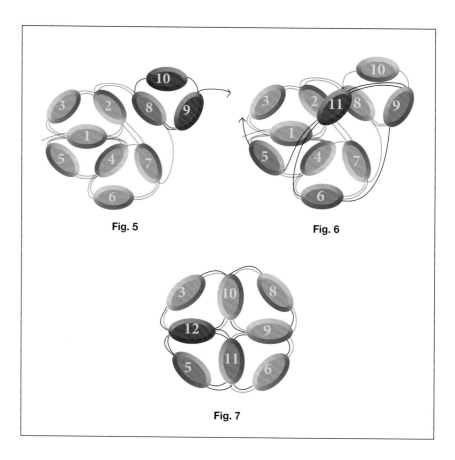

Fig. 5

Fig. 6

Fig. 7

Getting my beaded beads to feel appropriately solid and stiff has always been a challenge. Even after I had gone back around the bead path so many times I couldn't get the needle through one more time, sometimes the beads still felt a little squishy. I found the answer to my problem in an episode of Katie Hacker's PBS show "Beads, Baubles and Jewels." Guest Jean Campbell applied acrylic floor finish to her beading to stiffen the thread and, as a bonus, add a protective sheen to the beads.

5. Pick up beads 9 and 10. Sew through beads 8, 9, 10, 8, and 9 **(fig. 5)**.

6. Pick up bead 11. Sew through beads 6, 9, 11, and 5 **(fig. 6)**.

7. Pick up bead 12 and sew through bead 11. Reinforce the bead by going through all of the pinch beads (following the bead path) until you run out of thread or you can't get the needle through the beads any more. See the Tip on this page for an easy way to further stiffen the beaded bead **(fig. 7)**.

Chain necklace

1. Follow the beaded-bead directions to make three beads. Use the beads to make three bead units. For each one, on a headpin, string a 4mm round bead, a beaded bead, a 4mm round, and a pinch bead. Then make a plain loop (Basics, p. 102).

2. Cut three small pieces of chain: 1½-in. (3.8cm), 1-in. (2.5cm), and ½-in. (1.3cm) long. Attach a chain to each plain loop. Cut two 9-in. (23cm) pieces of chain. Use a jump ring (Basics, p. 103) to attach the three bead dangles and the two 9-in. chains.

3. On one chain end, attach a lobster claw clasp. (The chain I used had an attached loop. If yours doesn't have a loop, add a jump ring.) Attach a jump ring to the end of the second chain.

Earrings

Follow step 1 of the chain necklace and make a bead unit. Attach a two-link piece of chain to the plain loop. Open the loop of an earring wire, attach the dangle, and close the loop. Repeat to make a second earring.

COLOR CHOICES

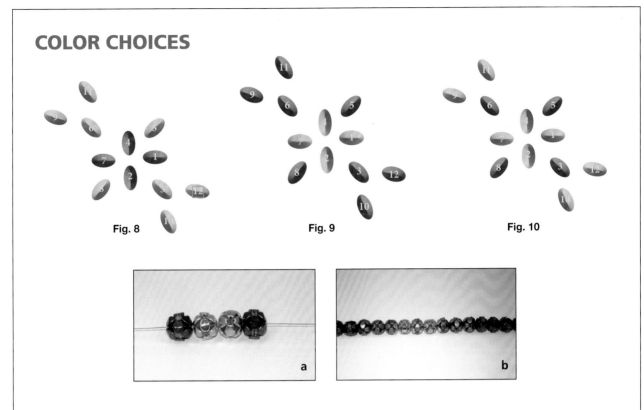

Fig. 8   Fig. 9   Fig. 10

a   b

By adding a second bead color at specific points in the woven bead, the effect of a small (or large) bead cap can be created. Another arrangement will create a stripe.
• In **Figure 8**, the purple beads create a small bead cap.
• In **Figure 9**, the purple beads create a large bead cap.
• In **Figure 10**, the purple beads create a stripe down the middle.

I used the small bead cap and stripe technique to create a flow of one color to another in the strung necklace. Initially, I was planning to use gold beaded beads as an accent to the blue beads. I found the difference between the colors too abrupt, but pairing the blue with the bronze wasn't distinct enough. After some experimentation, I settled on a flow of blue to bronze to gold and back again for just the right amount of pop **(photos a, b)**.

Beginner stitchers: For easier weaving, condition your thread by pulling it through some beading wax (such as Thread Heaven). This is particularly important when you're making multiple passes through the same bead.

...add more beads!

Beaded necklace

To string the beaded necklace, follow the beaded-bead directions and make 27–31 beads. Cut a 22-in. (56cm) piece of beading wire and string an alternating pattern of beaded beads, bicones, and gold and bronze pinch beads as shown (see Color Choices, p. 13). When you're done stringing, check the fit (allowing for 1–1½ in./2.5–3.7cm for finishing) and add or remove beads as necessary. On each end, string a crimp bead, a bicone, and half of a clasp. Go back through the beads just strung and tighten the wire. Crimp the crimp bead (Basics, p. 103) and trim the excess wire.

Necklace, 16 in. (41cm)

- **27–31** beaded beads
- **12–14** 6mm bicone crystals
- **18** 5x3mm pinch beads
- Flexible beading wire, .014
- **2** crimp beads
- Toggle clasp
- Diagonal wire cutters
- Chainnose or crimping pliers

Color Guide

Pinch beads: green iris, gold, and bronze

6mm bicone crystals: Montana

Lush loops

Adding something extra to a simply-strung necklace doesn't have to be complicated—or expensive. These lush loops do the trick. Plus, the circular, overlapping looping action can be a calming, zen activity after a frazzled day. Playing with color combinations can change the tone of the piece from everyday to black tie.

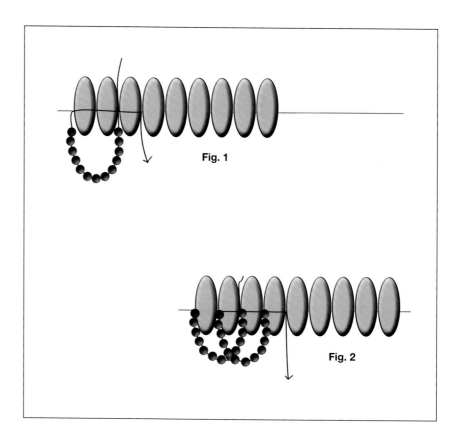

Fig. 1

Fig. 2

TIP

Check the length of the necklace before adding the loops (allowing for the clasp).

TIP

For the graduated loops, I counted to the center of the necklace and then divided the loop length accordingly. On each end, I made: ten 10-bead loops, ten 12-bead loops, ten 14-bead loops, ten 16-bead loops, and nine 18-bead loops. The center loop is 20 beads long.

TIP

For this necklace, I gradually made the loops longer as I moved to the center of the necklace, then decreased the length of the loops as I moved away from the center.

Necklace

1. Cut a 25-in. (64cm) piece of beading wire and string rondelles until the strand is the desired length. Add a bead stopper or a piece of tape to each end. Tie one end of a 36-in. (.9m) piece of conditioned thread to the beading wire between the second and third rondelle with two overhand knots (Basics, p. 104), leaving a 4-in. (10cm) tail. Thread a needle on the other end.

2. Pick up a loop of seed beads (see tip). Go back two rondelles and bring the thread through those two rondelles and the next rondelle **(fig. 1)**. Continue stringing loops of seed beads, repeating the two-rondelles-back-and-three-ahead pattern **(fig. 2)** until you reach the opposite end of the strand.

a

3. On each end, string a crimp bead and half of a clasp over the beading wire and the thread. Go back through the crimp bead and a couple of adjacent rondelles. Tighten the beading wire and thread. Crimp the crimp bead and tie the thread around the wire with two overhand knots **(photo a)**. Trim the wire and thread.

...loop it up!

Bracelet

1. Use heavy-duty wire cutters to cut 2½ coils of memory wire. On one end, use roundnose pliers to make a loop. String rondelles to the end of the coils; make another loop.

2. Follow the necklace instructions to make the seed bead loops. (For the bracelet, I didn't count the beads for each loop to achieve a fluffy, slightly uneven look.) Tie the thread off with overhand knots when you reach the second loop. Bring the thread back through a few rondelles and trim the threads on both ends. Hide the ends in the rondelles.

3. Tighten the second loop if necessary, so the rondelles are snug against each other **(photo b)**. If you end up with multiple loops, trim the wire to one loop with the heavy-duty wire cutters.

Supplies

Necklace, 19 in. (48cm)
- **90–100** 7mm glass rondelles
- 3g $8^{\underline{o}}$ seed beads, color A
- 5g $8^{\underline{o}}$ seed beads, color B
- **2** crimp beads
- Toggle clasp
- Beading thread
- Flexible beading wire, .012
- Beading needles, #10–#12
- Thread conditioner
- Scissors
- Roundnose pliers and chainnose pliers
- Diagonal wire cutters
- Bead stoppers or tape

Bracelet, 19 in. (48cm)
- **70–80** 7mm glass rondelles
- 5g $8^{\underline{o}}$ and $11^{\underline{o}}$ seed beads, various colors
- Memory wire
- Beading thread
- Flexible beading wire, .012
- Beading needles, #10–#12
- Thread conditioner
- Scissors
- Roundnose pliers and chainnose pliers
- Heavy-duty wire cutters

Color guide
Glass rondelles: purple pink mix opaque transparent Picasso
Seed beads: matte purple and transparent golden peach

...play with color combinations!

Easy earrings

You can make a simple pair of
earrings with the techniques used to
make the necklace or bracelets. For
each earring, slide three rondelles on
an earring hoop. You just make two
loops of seed beads—or more, if you
start with a large hoop and you don't
mind the extra weight.

Earrings

- **6** 7mm rondelles
- 2g 8º–11º seed beads
- Beading thread
- Pair of hoop-style
  earring wires
- Beading needles, #10–#12
- Thread conditioner
- Scissors

Circular logic

I can't decide whether these components remind me more of quilt segments or small firework bursts. In the end, the interpretations may be as varied as their uses. They work as separate elements or can be creatively linked. Luckily, they stitch up in a flash, so you'll have plenty of time to experiment.

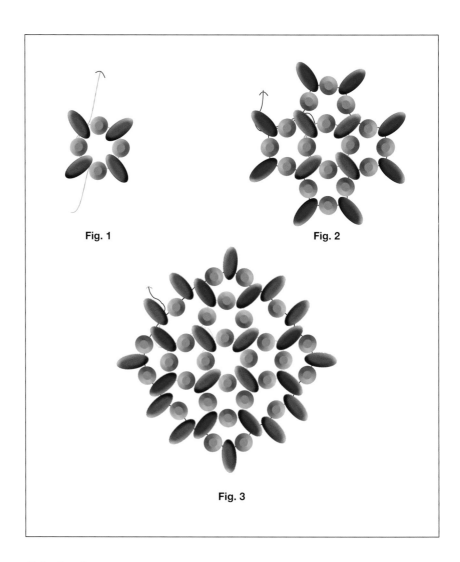

Fig. 1

Fig. 2

Fig. 3

ABOUT CHAIN

Chain with unsoldered links works best for the necklace because it is easy to remove links with two pairs of pliers, opening them like jump rings. You can also remove links from soldered chain, but you'll have to sacrifice one link for every one you cut off with wire cutters. Make sure you have a long enough chain before you start.

Stitched component

1. Thread a needle on one end of an 18-in. (46cm) piece of conditioned beading thread (Basics, p. 104). Working clockwise, pick up an alternating pattern of four 11º seed beads and four color A Twin beads. Tighten the beads into a circle and tie an overhand knot (Basics, p. 104). Sew through an A, an 11º, and an A **(fig. 1)**.

2. Bring the thread through the second hole of the Twin you just exited. Now going counter-clockwise, pick up an 11º, a color B Twin, an 11º, a B, an 11º, and the outer hole of the next A. Continue around until you finish the circle, and sew through the next 11º and B. Bring the thread through the second hole of the B you just exited **(fig. 2)**.

3. Going clockwise again, pick up an A, an 11º, an A, and the outer hole of the next B. Then pick up an 11º, an A, an 11º, and the outer hole of the next B. Continue around until you finish the circle. Sew through the next A **(fig. 3)** and bring the thread through the second hole of the A you just exited.

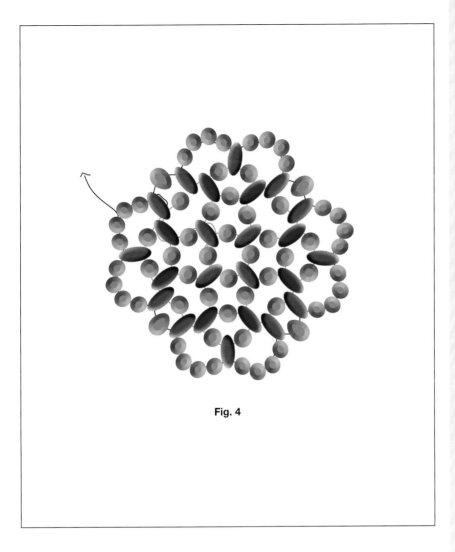

Fig. 4

4. Going counterclockwise, pick up four 11°s, the outer hole on an A, four 11°s, the outer hole of an A, a drop bead, and the outer hole of the A. Continue around until you finish the circle. Sew through a few of the next beads, tie an overhand knot, and trim the thread. Make a total of four stitched components **(fig. 4)**.

Chain necklace
Cut a 18-in. (46cm) piece of chain. From the remaining chain, separate three more individual links. Using jump rings (Basics, p. 103), attach an alternation pattern of four stitched components and three chain links.

Use the remaining two jump rings to attach each end of the chain to a stitched component. (The necklace does not have a clasp. This length went over my head without a problem, but be sure to test the length and err on the long side.)

Earrings
Make two stitched components. Use jump rings to attach them to earring wires.

Supplies
Chain necklace, 24 in. (61cm)
- **64** Twin (or SuperDuo) beads, color A
- **32** Twin (or SuperDuo) beads, color B
- **16** 3.4mm drop beads
- 1g 11° seed beads
- Beading thread
- 18 in. (46cm) chain, plus three links
- **8** 7mm jump rings
- Beading needles, #10–#12
- Thread conditioner
- Roundnose and chainnose pliers or two pairs of chainnose pliers
- Diagonal wire cutters

Earrings
- **32** Twin (or SuperDuo) beads, color A
- **16** Twin (or SuperDuo) beads, color B
- **8** 3.4mm drop beads
- 1g 11° seed beads, copper
- Beading thread
- **2** 7mm jump rings
- Pair of earring wires
- Beading needles, #10 or #12
- Thread conditioner
- Roundnose and chainnose pliers
- Diagonal wire cutters

Color Guide
Color A Twins: dark teal
Color B Twins: matte neon blue
11° seed beads: matte copper
Drops: copper

Connected necklace

For a different look, I added more drop beads to the outer rows, strategically substituting a Twin now and then to link two components together without the use of a jump ring. If you choose the non-jump ring route, sketch out the arrangement before you start stitching because the Twin beads are part of each of the components they link. So, you'll be attaching the components to each other as you create them. This takes a little extra focus. I had to backtrack a few times with this necklace after realizing I linked two components at the wrong place.

Necklace, 18 in. (46cm)

- **120** Twin (or SuperDuo) beads, color A
- **60** Twin (or SuperDuo) beads, color B
- **32** 3.4mm drop beads
- 2g 11° seed beads
- Beading thread
- **4** 7mm jump rings
- 18 in. (46cm) chain
- Beading needles, #10–#12
- Thread conditioner
- Roundnose and chainnose pliers, or two pairs of chainnose pliers
- Diagonal wire cutters

Color Guide
Color A Twins: dark teal
Color B Twins: turquoise
11° seed beads: transparent dark teal
Drops: turquoise/copper

Grasping at (colorful) straws

Stitch peyote straws in slightly different lengths and diameters to add color and swing to your jewelry. Using the same technique, I chose Mardi Gras colors for the necklace and a moodier, more sophisticated palette for the bracelet. I picked something from each color scheme for the *done-in-a-flash* earrings. If you're looking for a beginner peyote project or are just in a short-attention-span place, this is a perfect project to stitch up.

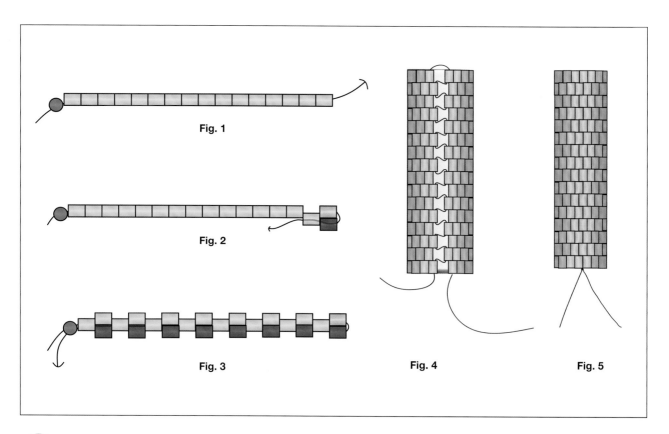

Fig. 1

Fig. 2

Fig. 3

Fig. 4

Fig. 5

TIP

I didn't have 8mm bicones in cyclamen for the necklace, so I used top-drilled pendants. Instead of using a headpin, I

strung the pendant off-center on a piece of 24-gauge wire, folding up the ends. Then I strung the straw and top crystal and made the loop with the longer end.

Make the straws

(The necklace uses three sizes of straws: 16 beads x 8 beads, 12x6, and 8x6.)

1. For the 16x8 straw, thread a needle on one end of a 28-in. (71cm) piece of conditioned thread. Attach a stop bead about 10 in. (25cm) from the end (Basics, p. 104). Pick up 16 11º cylinder beads **(fig. 1)**.

2. Pick up an 11º. Skip the last bead picked up and sew through the next bead in the row **(fig. 2)**.

3. Pick up another 11º, skip a bead, and sew through the next bead. Continue until your thread is exiting the last bead in the row **(fig. 3)**.

4. Start each new row by picking up an 11º and skipping and passing through the first raised bead, which will be the last bead added in the previous row. Continue until you have finished eight rows.

5. Remove the stop bead and thread the needle on the 10-in. thread. Bring

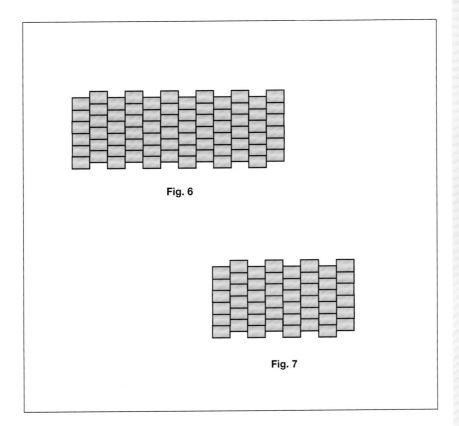

Fig. 6

Fig. 7

the sides together so the edge beads fit together like a zipper. Sew in and out of the raised edge beads as shown **(fig. 4)**. Tighten the thread and tie the ends together in an overhand knot (Basics, p. 104). **(fig. 5)**. Make a total of three 16x8 straws, ten 12x6 straws, and two 8x6 straws **(fig. 6, 7)**.

Necklace

1. First, put together the straw dangles. For each dangle, string a crystal, a straw, and a crystal on a headpin. Make the first half of a wrapped loop (Basics, p. 102). Cut a 20-in. (51cm) piece of chain. Center a large dangle on the center link of the chain and complete the wrapped loop. On each end, attach a medium dangle, a large dangle, four medium dangles, and a small dangle, completing the loops as you go.

2. On one end, use a jump ring (Basics, p. 103) to attach the lobster claw clasp. Then, attach a jump ring to the opposite end of the chain.

Supplies

Necklace, 21 in. (53cm)
- **30** 4–8mm bicone crystals and crystal rondelles
- 5g 11º cylinder beads
- 3–4mm stop bead
- 20 in. (51cm) chain
- **15** 3-in. (7.6cm) headpins
- **2** 7mm jump rings
- Lobster-claw clasp
- Beading thread
- Beading needles, #10–#12
- Thread conditioner
- Roundnose pliers and chainnose pliers
- Diagonal wire cutters

Bracelet, 7½ in. (19cm)
- **2** 14mm fancy silver beads
- **8–10** 10mm fire-polished rondelles
- 5g 11º cylinder beads
- **22–24** 8mm fire-polished beads
- **22–24** 6mm round spacer beads
- 3–4mm stop bead
- 3 in. (7.6cm) 22-gauge wire
- 5 in. (13cm) chain
- **30–32** 3-in. (7.6cm) headpins
- 10mm oval jump ring
- Toggle clasp
- Beading thread
- Beading needles, #10–#12

Color Guide
necklace
11º cylinder beads: luminous dusky blue Delicas
crystals: amethyst, cyclamen Indian pink, indicolite, olivine, and tangerine

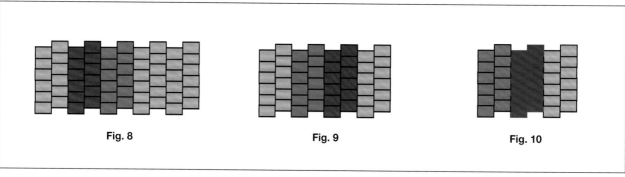

| Fig. 8 | Fig. 9 | Fig. 10 |

Bracelet

1. Follow straw steps 1–5 to stitch six 10x6, six 8x6, and six 6x6 straws, according to these color patterns **(fig. 8–10)**. For each dangle, string a silver spacer, a tube, and a fire-polished bead or rondelle on a headpin. Make the first half of a wrapped loop (Basics, p. 102).

2. To create the focal bead segment, cut a 3-in. (7.6cm) piece of 22-gauge wire. Make the first half of a wrapped loop. String a rondelle, a focal bead, a silver spacer, a focal, and a rondelle. Make the first half of a wrapped loop.

3. Attach the loop half of a toggle clasp to one end of the focal segment, and finish the loop. Cut a 5-in. (13cm) piece of chain and attach it to the other end of the segment. On the opposite end of the chain, attach the toggle half of the clasp with a jump ring (Basics, p. 103).

4. Attach three dangles of different sizes to each of the first five links of chain nearest the focal segment, finishing the wrapped loops as you go.

5. Make 14 smaller bead units by stringing a fire-polished bead on a headpin and making the first half of a wrapped loop. Attach three bunches of three bead units each to the chain between the toggle and the dangles. Attach the other five units to the chain among the dangles.

...enjoy simple, easy style!

Earrings

For each earring, make a tube dangle and stack it on a headpin with silver beads and seed beads. Make a wrapped loop (Basics, p. 102) and attach the loop to an earring wire.

Earrings
- **2** tube dangles
- **2** 3-in. (7.6cm) headpins
- Assorted silver beads and seed beads
- Chainnose pliers and roundnose pliers
- Diagonal wire cutters

Color Guide
11º cylinder beads:
opaque steel gray, semi-matte transparent silver-lined light silver gray, and dark lavender Delicas

Twin spins

Working two-hole Twin beads into basic circles can offer a new spin on a classic beaded-bead design. Flipping up a Twin can turn your bead into an earring or pendant, while stacking layers of Twins can give bracelet sliders an extra bit of dimension.

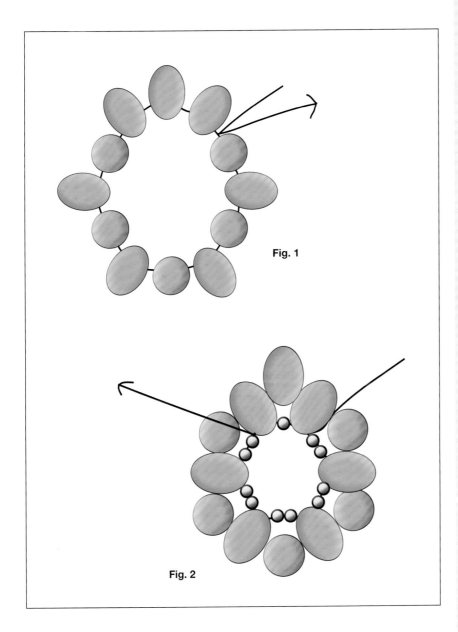

Fig. 1

Fig. 2

Supplies

Pendant (or one earring)
- **5** 4mm bicone crystals
- **7** Twin (or SuperDuo) beads
- **11** 13º Charlotte seed beads
- Beading thread
- Beading needles, #10–#12
- Thread conditioner
- Scissors

Bracelet (two short sliders and one tall)
- **24** 4mm fire-polished round beads
- **32** Twin (or SuperDuo) beads
- **6** 12mm twisted bugle beads
- 1g 13º Charlottes
- 7–8 in. (18–20cm) of ½-in. (1.3cm) leather
- Magnetic clasp
- Beading thread
- Beading needles, #10–#12
- Thread conditioner
- Two-part epoxy
- Scissors

Color Guide
Bracelet
Twin beads: turquoise
fire-polished rounds: opaque white

Necklace and earrings
crystals: fire opal AB
Twin beads: yellow-orange pearls

Pendant/Earrings

1. Thread a needle on one end of an 8-in. (20cm) piece of conditioned thread (Basics, p. 104). Pick up three Twin beads and an alternating pattern of five 4mm bicones and four Twin beads. Tighten the beads into a circle and tie an overhand knot **(fig. 1)**.

2. Flip all the Twins so they are pointing to the center of the circle, except the middle Twin in the set of three. Bring the thread through the inner hole of the Twin closest to the knot. Pick up a Charlotte and the inner hole of the next Twin. Continue to pick up two Charlottes between each subsequent Twin until you complete the circle. Sew through the inner circle again to snug up the beads **(fig. 2)**. Tie an overhand knot (Basics, p. 104). Trim the thread.

3. Attach a 7mm 24-gauge jump ring to the free hole of the top Twin and string the pendant on a fine chain or bead strand. For earrings, make two pendants and attach them to 1-in. (3.5cm) chains with 24-gauge jump rings, then attach the dangle to earring wires.

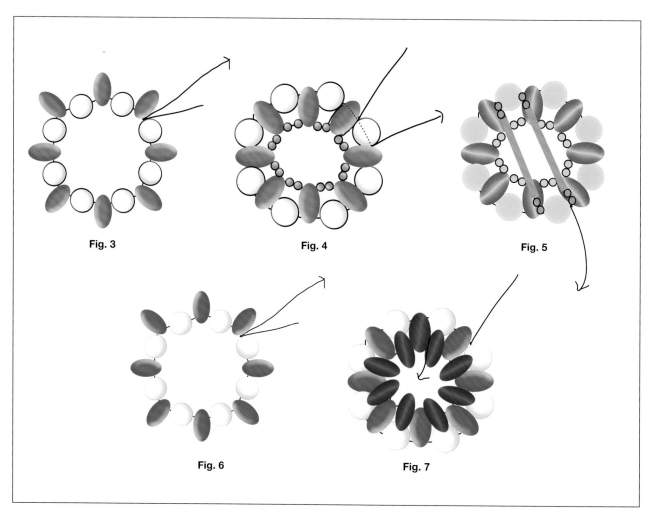

Fig. 3

Fig. 4

Fig. 5

Fig. 6

Fig. 7

Replacing a bicone with another flipped Twin bead will turn a pendant into a link.

Bracelet
Short slider

1. Thread a needle on one end of a 12-in. (30cm) piece of conditioned thread. Working clockwise, pick up an alternating pattern of eight 4mm fire-polished beads and eight Twin beads. Tighten the beads into a circle and tie an overhand knot (Basics, p. 104) **(fig. 3)**.

2. Flip the Twins so they are pointing toward the center of the circle. Working counterclockwise, sew through the inner hole of the Twin closest to the knot. Pick up two Charlottes and then sew through the inner hole of the next Twin. Continue to pick up two Charlottes between each Twin until you complete the circle. Sew through the inner circle again to snug up the beads. Bring the thread back to the outer hole on the left side of the nearest Twin. Sew back through the Twin and the adjacent 4mm round **(fig. 4)**.

3. Pick up two Charlottes, a bugle bead, and two Charlottes. Bring the beads across the back of the beaded unit and through the opposite 4mm bead. Pick up two Charlottes, a bugle bead, and two Charlottes, and then sew through the original 4mm. Sew through all the beads in this step again, and tie an overhand knot next to the last 4mm. Trim the thread **(fig. 5)**.

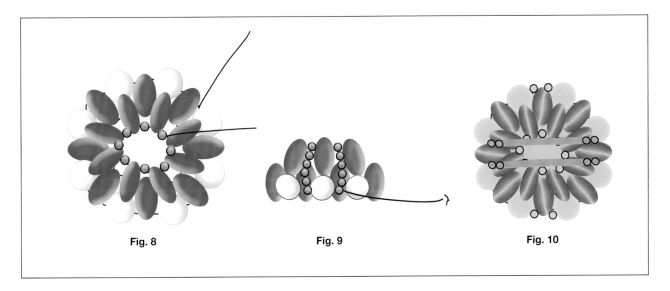

Fig. 8   Fig. 9   Fig. 10

Tall slider

1. Thread a needle on one end of a 12-in. (30cm) piece of conditioned thread. Working clockwise, pick up an alternating pattern of eight 4mm fire-polished beads and eight Twin beads. Tighten the beads into a circle and tie an overhand knot (Basics, p. 104) **(fig. 6)**.

2. Flip the Twins so they are pointing toward the center of the circle. Working counterclockwise, sew through the inner hole of the Twin closest to the knot. Pick up a new Twin and sew through the inner hole of the next Twin in the circle. Continue to pick up new Twins between each already-strung Twin until you complete a new circle. Sew through the circle again to snug up the beads **(fig. 7)**.

3. Flip the new Twins so they are pointing toward the center of the circle. Working clockwise, bring the thread through the inner hole of the closest inner Twin. Pick up a Charlotte and the inner hole of the next Twin. Continue to add a Charlotte between each Twin until you complete the circle. Sew through the inner circle again to snug up the beads **(fig. 8)**.

4. With the thread exiting a Charlotte, pick up enough new Charlottes (seven or eight) to reach the hole of the 4mm round beneath the original Charlotte in the circle. Sew through the round, string seven or eight new Charlottes, and sew through the next Charlotte in the inner ring. Bring the thread to the opposite side of the inner circle and repeat **(fig. 9)**.

5. Follow step 4 of the short slider to add the bugle beads. Make sure they are perpendicular to the accents added in step 4 of the tall slider **(fig. 10)**.

Assembly

Cut the piece of leather ½ in. (1.3cm) shorter than the finished length (to allow for the clasp). Center the sliders over the leather in the desired order, making sure the bugle beads are against the inside of the leather. Mix two-part epoxy according to the package directions and attach half of the clasp to each side of the leather. Allow the epoxy to dry **(photo)**.

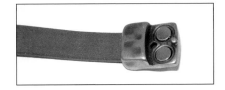

 TIP

Since bits of thread will be visible when you step up (or in) to the next ring, choose clear Fireline or a color that will blend into your Twins.

Princess charming

I had some fun creating pendant charms in simple color combinations to represent eight favorite Disney princesses. These palettes are pretty obvious, but with a bit of imagination, you could create charms to represent any number of fictional and real-life heroines. Check out my Facebook page (www.facebook.com/BeadingInsider) for the royal color combos.

Painting with beads

The bead embroidery masterpieces of artists such as Sherry
Serafini, Jaime Cloud Eakin, and Kinga Nichols are gorgeous—
and sometimes a bit daunting in their intricacy. But there are plenty
of ways to dip your creative toe into this potentially addictive
technique. One leftover vacation coin (or an interesting button) can
be your admission into this colorful world. After that, how far you
travel into bead embroidery is up to you.

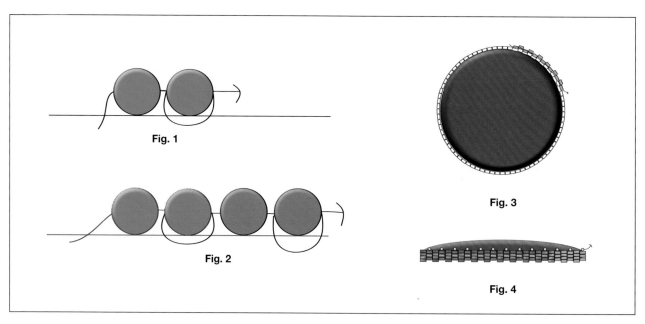

Fig. 1

Fig. 2

Fig. 3

Fig. 4

a

b

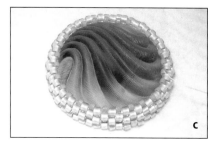

c

Button bracelet

1. Sketch at least a general idea of your design on a piece of paper. Cut a piece of Stiff Stuff at least ½ in. (1.3cm) larger all around your design. Because my bracelet blank has an open back, I didn't need to remove the shank of the button, but I did need to cut a small hole in the Stiff Stuff so the button could lay flat **(photo a)**. Glue the button onto the Stiff Stuff. Let the glue dry. Draw a faint outline of the design on the material with a pencil **(photo b)**.

2. Thread 36 in. (.9m) of conditioned thread on the needle. Tie an overhand knot (Basics, p. 104) on the opposite end. From the back, sew up through the foundation next to the button. Pick up two 11º cylinder beads and sew down through the foundation. Bring the needle up between the two 11ºs and sew through the last 11º picked up **(fig. 1)**.

3. Pick up two more 11ºs and sew down through the foundation. Bring the needle up between the two 11ºs and sew through the last 11º picked up **(fig. 2)**. Continue until you complete a circle around the button. Sew through the beads in the circle again to snug up the beads.

4. To build the peyote stitch bezel wall, pick up an 11º, skip the first bead in the circle, and sew through the next 11º **(fig. 3)**. Continue working in peyote stitch (Basics, p. 105) to complete the round. Step up for the next row by picking up a bead and sewing through the first raised bead.

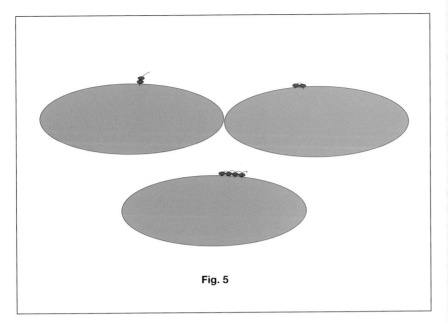

Fig. 5

Supplies
Button bracelet
- 32mm cabochon or button
- 3–4g 8º and 11º seed beads in various colors
- 1g 11º cylinder beads
- **30–40** 15º cylinder beads
- **2** 6mm fire-polished oval beads
- Beading thread
- Beading needles, #10–#12
- Thread conditioner
- Ultrasuede
- Lacy's Stiff Stuff beading foundation
- E6000 adhesive
- Scissors
- Cuff blank

Color Guide
11º cylinder beads: silver-lined white Delicas
15º cylinder beads: matte seafoam and metallic gold Delicas
15º round seed beads: dark teal

5. Continue stitching to add as many rows as is necessary to reach the height of the button. For the top row (which will cradle the button), switch to 15º cylinder beads. Work the thread back down through the beads to the back of the foundation **(fig. 4, photo c)**.

6. I began embroidering my design by backstitching another circle of 11º cylinders around the button, sewing a 6mm bead on each side, and backstitching three rows around them. I also added a row of backstitch around the edge of my final shape to create a border on my design. For this bracelet, I decided on the rest of the design as I went along, but if you're planning something more complicated with a wider range of beads, you'll probably want to sketch a plan **(photo d)**.

7. Glue your embroidered oval to a piece of Ultrasuede. I did not trim around the Stiff Stuff edge first because I would make the layers the same size by trimming them together **(photo e)**.

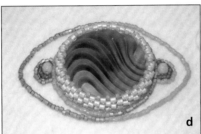

d

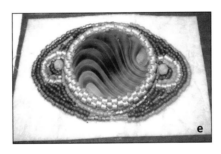

e

8. Adding a beaded edge gives the piece a more finished look. To add a brick stitch edge, start a new thread as you did in step 1, but start from the front, hiding the knot under the beads near the edge of the design and bringing the thread out between the two layers and back up through the Stiff Stuff at the edge of the beadwork **(fig. 5)**.

TIP

Finish each thread by bringing the needle through the Stiff Stuff, tying two or three knots as close to the back of the fabric as possible and trimming the thread. You can add a tiny drop of adhesive to the knot for extra security. Start each new thread as in step 1.

f

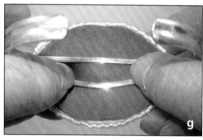

g

10. Pick up two 11º cylinders and sew through both layers. Before tightening the beads to the base, bring the thread down through the second bead. Tighten the thread. Pick up another 11º, sew down through both layers again, and exit through the same bead **(photo f)**. Continue around the oval until you reach the first bead. Bring the thread down through the first bead to finish the oval. Weave the needle back though the beadwork, tying two or three knots as you go, always hiding them under the beads. Trim the thread.

11. To attach the embroidered component to the bracelet blank, add adhesive to the blank and center the component. I GENTLY used a pair of butterfly clips to hold the pieces in place while the glue dried. If you use the quicker-setting adhesive (two-part epoxy), you can hold it in place while it dries **(photo g)**.

Easy earrings

To make earrings, I secured a small cab to the backing and skipped the bezel entirely. I just did a simple backstich around the oval, with one, three-bead picot. Even the edging seemed too much, so the back of the earring is unfinished. Since the earrings were for me, I left it at that, but if I wanted to give or sell them, I would have cut ovals of backing and Ultrasuede before I started beading and whip-stitched (Basics, p. 106) them together. Then I would have glued the cab and done the backstitching.

...spotlight a coin instead!

Consider mixing finishes (matte, transparent, etc.) and shapes as well as colors when creating your embroidery. For the coin bezel, I used only black but mixed matte cylinder beads with glossy round beads.

Coin bracelet

Make the same as the button bracelet, following step 1–3 and 8–11 (skipping steps 4–7).

Bracelet
- 20mm coin
- 1g 11º cylinder beads
- **30–40** 11º round seed beads
- Beading thread
- Beading needles, #10–#12
- Thread conditioner
- Ultrasuede
- E6000 adhesive
- Lacy's Stiff Stuff beading foundation
- Scissors
- Cuff blank

Color Guide
11º cylinder beads: black matte Delicas
11º seed beads: black and transparent

Style in the round

When I see a ring component (or a washer from the hardware store), I always hear it begging for embellishment. A couple of rows of brick stitch turn these simple circles into colorful pinwheels. Add some linking Tila beads and you have the start of some quick and chic jewelry.

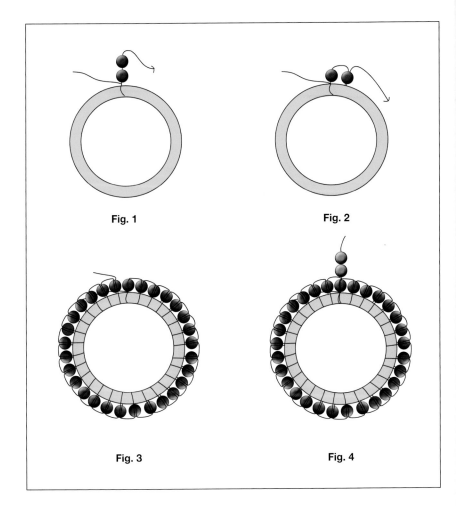

Fig. 1

Fig. 2

Fig. 3

Fig. 4

Supplies

Necklace, 21 in. (53cm)

- **3** 18mm rings
- **3** Tila beads
- 2g 11º cylinder beads, in two colors
- **30–40** 11º seed beads
- 20 in. (51cm) 2mm link chain
- **2** crimp beads
- 7mm jump ring
- 4mm jump ring
- Spring-ring clasp
- 5–6 in. (13–15cm) flexible beading wire
- Beading thread
- Beading needles, #10–#12
- **2** pairs of chainnose pliers
- Crimping pliers (optional)
- Diagonal wire cutters
- Thread conditioner
- Scissors
- Bead stopper or tape

Bracelet, 7½ in. (19cm)

- **6** 18mm rings
- **6** Tila beads
- 6g 11º cylinder beads, in two colors
- 10mm jump ring (optional)
- 18mm lobster claw clasp
- Beading thread
- Beading needles, #10–#12
- Thread conditioner
- Scissors

Color Guide
Necklace
11º cylinder beads: light orchid Ceylon and opaque luster purple Delicas
Tila beads: opaque matte violet blue luster

Bracelet
11º cylinder beads: luminous dusk blue and transparent luster tropical teal Delicas
Tila beads: semi-matte metallic aquamarine rainbow

Necklace pinwheels

1. Thread a needle on a 36-in. (.9m) piece of conditioned beading thread, and tie the other end around a ring component with a surgeon's knot (Basics, p. 104), leaving a 6-in. (15cm) tail. Pick up two 11º cylinder beads. Note: I alternated between two colors around each row **(fig. 1)**.

2. Bring the thread behind and through the center of the ring and back through the last bead picked up. Tighten the thread to nestle the beads next to each other **(fig. 2)**.

3. Pick up an 11º cylinder and repeat step 2 until you complete the row **(fig. 3)**.

4. Pass the needle down through the first bead picked up. Bring the thread behind and through the center of the ring and back through the bead. You'll start the second row from here by picking up two 11º cylinders **(fig. 4)**.

5. Sew under the nearest thread loop in the previous row. Pull the thread tight.

The thread will show around the ring components, but it becomes part of the design. It's a good idea to coordinate the thread color with the beads, even though the color is barely visible. It's the extra attention to detail that elevates a good design to great.

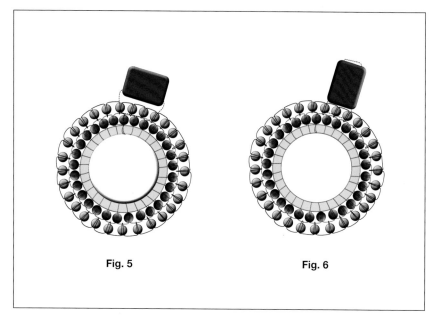

Fig. 5   Fig. 6

6. Pick up an 11° cylinder and repeat step 2 (going through the first row thread loops instead of going around the ring) until you complete the row. When the row is completed, repeat step 4, linking the first and last beads. Pick up one hole of a Tila bead and sew through the cylinder underneath **(fig. 5)**. Tighten the thread and sew through the circle again. Weave the thread back through the beadwork and trim the thread. Thread the needle on the 6-in. tail. Weave the tail back through the beadwork and trim the thread. Make a total of three pinwheel components.

Necklace

1. Cut two 1-in. (2.5cm) pieces of chain and two 9-in. (23cm) pieces of chain, and set them aside. (This will result in a 21-in. (53cm) necklace. Adjust the 9-in. pieces to change the length of the finished necklace.) Cut a 6-in. piece of flexible beading wire. On the wire, string: a crimp bead, a pinwheel component (the top Tila hole), the first link of a 1-in. chain, 1 in. of 11° seed beads, the last link of the chain, a pinwheel, the first link of a second 1-in. chain, 1 in. of 11° seed beads, the last link of the second chain, a pinwheel, and a crimp bead.

2. Secure one end of the segment with a bead stopper or tape. On the

 TIP

I used tornado instead of regular crimps in the necklace because the ridges in the tornados echoed the thread design again the rings. If you use any kind of ridged crimp beads, you can omit crimping pliers from your tool list.

other end, string an end link of a 9-in. piece of chain. Go back through the crimp bead and the adjacent Tila hole. Tighten the wire and crimp the crimp bead (Basics, p. 103). Trim the excess wire. On the other end, remove the bead stopper or tape and repeat. Attach a clasp to one end of the chain with a 4mm jump ring. Attach a 7mm jump ring to the other end.

Bracelet

1. When making pinwheels for the bracelet, you'll attach the Tilas so they are parallel with the cylinder beads. Link the units by sewing the Tila of the first unit into the second unit and so on.

2. For the final pinwheel, use a larger length of thread if necessary to ensure you have 12 in. (30 cm) left over. Do not weave it back into the beads. You'll still weave in the tail.

3. To add the clasp, thread the needle back on to the working thread of the final pinwheel. Pick up 9 or 10 11° cylinders and the loop of a clasp. Sew through the second Tila hole and tighten the thread. Tighten the thread and sew through the circle again. Weave the thread back through the beadwork and trim the thread.

4. On the opposite end of the bracelet, attach a 10mm jump ring (optional).

...stitch simple accessories!

TIP

The outer ring of the pinwheel is, of course, a little larger than the inner ring, so if you use the same number of cylinder beads, the spacing will be different. I like the slightly fanned out look, but if the inconsistency makes you nuts, you can add a bead (or two) to the outer ring, by passing through the same loop when you add the next bead at one or two points around the ring.

Earrings

For each earring, make a pinwheel component, omitting the Tilas. Use 10mm jump rings to attach the component to an earring wire (Basics, p. 103).

Earrings
- **2** 18mm rings
- **2g** 11º cylinder beads, in two colors
- Beading thread
- **2** 10mm jump rings
- Pair of earring wires
- Beading needles, #10–#12
- Thread conditioner

- **2** pairs of chainnose pliers
- Scissors

Color Guide
11º cylinder beads: light orchid Ceylon and opaque luster purple Delicas

Raising the bar

Cubic right-angle weave (CRAW) can be a bit challenging, but once you find the rhythm and can picture how the cubes are formed, you may find it addictive. I've seen stitchers use CRAW to form all kinds of interesting shapes, but even the simplest, quickest bars offer endless design possibilities. Everybody explains it a bit differently. Instead of being confusing, the more different ways I've heard it explained, the clearer it becomes to me. This is the simplest way for me to explain the process.

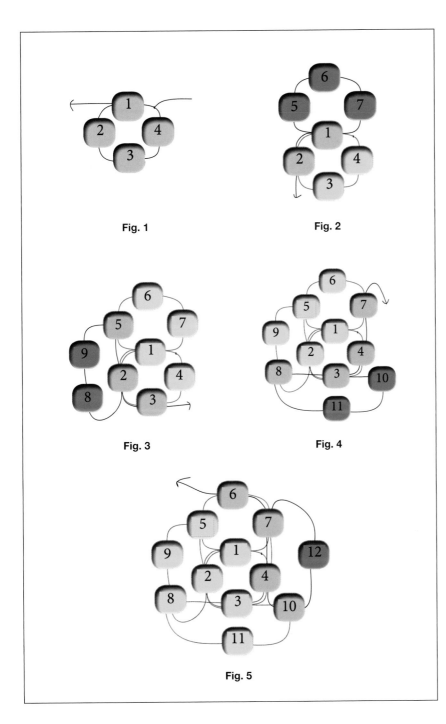

Fig. 1

Fig. 2

Fig. 3

Fig. 4

Fig. 5

Making a CRAW bar

1. Cut a 24-in. (61cm) piece of Fireline and thread a needle on one end. Pick up four cube beads and tie them into a ring with a square knot (Basics, p. 104). Sew through all four beads and the first bead again. This is the floor of the first cube of the bar **(fig. 1)**.

2. Pick up three beads (5, 6, and 7). Sew back through beads 1 and 2 **(fig. 2)**.

3. Pick up two beads (8 and 9). Sew back through beads 5, 2, and 3 **(fig. 3)**.

4. Pick up two beads (10 and 11). Sew back through beads 8, 3, 4, and 7 **(fig. 4)**.

5. Pick up one bead (12). Sew back through 10, 4, 7, and 6 **(fig. 5)**.

Supplies

Multiple bar necklace, 17 in. (43cm)

- 3g 8mm seed beads, color A
- 4g 8mm seed beads, color B
- Flexible beading wire, .014
- 7mm jump ring
- 7mm soldered jump ring
- **2** crimp beads
- Lobster claw clasp
- Fireline, 6 lb. test
- Beading needles, #10–#12
- Scissors
- Thread conditioner
- Diagonal wire cutters
- Chainnose pliers or crimping pliers

Pearl necklace, 16 in. (41cm)

- **18–22** 12mm coin pearls
- **2** 14mm coin pearls
- 2g 3mm cube beads
- 1g 11º cylinder beads
- **2** crimp beads
- Toggle clasp
- Flexible beading wire, .014
- Fireline, 6 lb. test
- Beading needles, #10–#12
- Scissors
- Thread conditioner
- Diagonal wire cutters
- Chainnose pliers or crimping pliers

Color Guide

12mm coin pearls: peach
14mm coin pearls: forest green
3mm cube beads: matte metallic khaki iris
11º cylinder beads: matte gold Delicas
8º seed beads: matte metallic khaki iris and transparent smoky amethyst

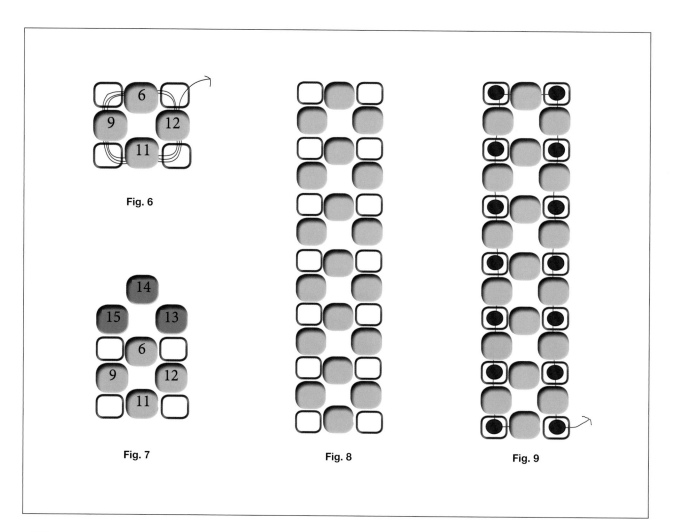

Fig. 6

Fig. 7

Fig. 8

Fig. 9

TIP

The first time you get to step 6 of "Making the bar," it may look like you have a random blob of beads: Which beads are the ceiling again? This will eventually go away as you become better at visualizing the structure, but to speed up the process, use different color for the walls. It's a good visual clue as to which beads you'll want to join for the ceiling. I used this method for some of the multicolored bars in the multiple bar necklace.

6. Cinch up the four ceiling beads (6, 12, 11, and 9). A solid base cube will make building the rest of the bar easier. Reinforce the cube, making sure to follow the thread path **(fig. 6)**.

7. Build the next cube by using the ceiling beads as the floor beads and following steps 2–5 **(fig. 7)**. Keep adding cubes until your bar is the desired length. In this necklace, the bar is six cubes long. Sew back through the thread paths to reinforce the structure until it feels solid. To end a thread, weave back into the beadwork, following the existing thread path and tying two or three half-hitch knots (Basics, p. 104) between beads as you go. Change directions as you weave so the thread crosses itself. Sew through a few beads after the last knot and trim the thread **(fig. 8)**.

Embellishment

To add the optional 11º cylinder bead embellishment, cut a 12-in. (30cm) piece of Fireline and thread a needle on one end. Sew through a few beads in the bar so the thread emerges from a bottom cube bead, pick up an 11º, and sew through the next cube on the side. Sew through each cube in the row, adding an 11º between each one. Sew through the top bead and add an 11º between each cube in the next row. Continue with the third and fourth row and then tie off the thread as in CRAW bar, step 7 **(fig. 9)**.

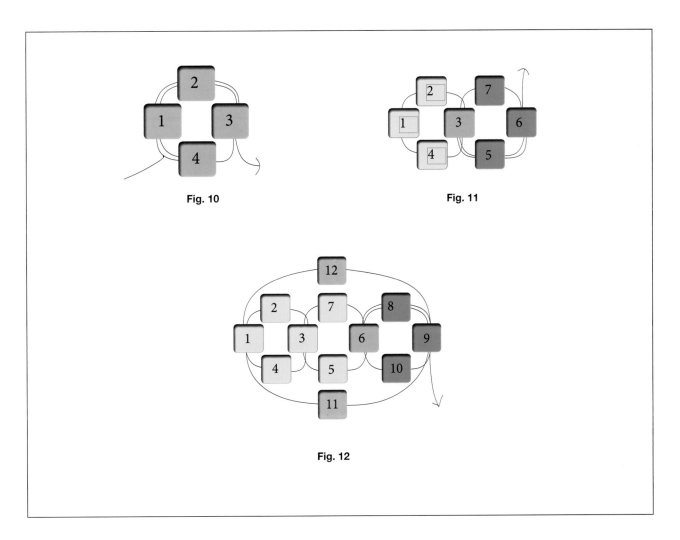

Fig. 10

Fig. 11

Fig. 12

Alternative method for bar

1. Cut a 24-in. (61cm) piece of Fire-line, and thread a needle on one end. Pick up four cube beads and tie them into a ring with a square knot (Basics, p. 104) **(fig. 10)**.

2. Pick up three beads (5, 6, and 7). Sew back through 3 and continue through 5 and 6 **(fig. 11)**.

3. Pick up three beads (8, 9, and 10). Sew back through 6 and continue through 8 and 9. Pick up a bead (11), and sew through 1. Pick up a bead (12), and sew through 9 **(fig. 12)**. Cinch up the four ceiling beads (11, 1, 12, and 9). Reinforce the cube, making sure to follow the thread path.

Add the second cube by following steps 2–5 of "Making a CRAW bar."

Multiple bar necklace

1. To make the multiple bar necklace, follow the directions for "Making a CRAW bar" to stitch one six-cube bar, two five-cube bars, four four-cube bars, two two-cube bars, and two one-cube bars with color A 8º seed beads. Stitch two five-cube bars and two one cube bars with color B 8º seed beads. Stitch two three-cube bars and two two-cube bars using a mix of As and Bs. For the mixed bars, use one color for the ceiling and floor and one for the walls (see Tips, p. 44).

2. Cut a 22-in. (56cm) piece of flexible beading wire. Center the bars as shown, stringing a color B 8º between each bar. On each end, string 8ºs until the strand is within ½ in. (1.3cm) of the finished length.

3. Use a jump ring (Basics, p. 103) to attach a lobster claw clasp. On one end, string a crimp bead, an 8º and the jump ring attached to the clasp. Repeat on the other end, substituting a soldered jump ring. Check the fit and add or remove beads as needed. On each end, go back through the beads just strung and tighten the wire. Crimp the crimp beads (Basics, p. 103) and trim the excess wire.

Pearl necklace

TIP

It's kind of counter intuitive, but I found cube beads to be a bit trickier than standard seed beads when working CRAW. They don't nestle as well. So if you're trying this stitch for the first time, you might find it easier to leave cubes for your second project.

Pearl necklace

1. Make a six-cube bar using 3mm cube beads for the celing and floor and 11º cylinder beads for the walls.

2. Cut a 22-in. (56cm) piece of flexible beading wire. Center 12 11ºs and center the top cube of the bar over the 11ºs. On each end, string 11ºs, cubes, and 12mm and 14mm coin pearls as shown until the strand is within ½ in. (1.3cm) of the finished length.

3. On each end, string a crimp bead and half of a clasp. Check the fit and add or remove cubes as needed. Go back through the beads just strung and tighten the wire. Crimp the crimp beads (Basics, p. 103) and trim the excess wire.

 TIP

Mixing finishes as well as colors adds visual interest to the multiple bar necklace. Color A is matte and color B is transparent.

...make an easy change!

Chain necklace

1. Follow the directions from "Making a CRAW bar" to stitch two five-cube bars and one four-cube bar with 3mm cube beads. Cut a 3-in. (7.6cm) piece of 22-gauge wire. On one end of the wire, make a plain loop (Basics, p. 102). String the second cube of the five-cube bar, a cube, the first cube of the four-cube bar, a cube, and the second cube of the five-cube bar. Make a plain loop.

2. Cut a 1-in. (2.5cm) piece of 22-gauge wire. Make a plain loop. String a pearl. Make a plain loop. Make a second pearl unit.

3. On each end, open a plain loop of the bar unit and attach a pearl unit. Cut a 3-in. (7.6cm) piece of chain. Attach one end of each chain to each free plain loop. Cut two 8½-in. (21.6cm) pieces of chain. Attach each chain to the same plain loops. On each end, use a jump ring (Basics, p. 103) to attach half of a clasp.

Chain necklace, 24 in. (61cm)

- **2** 14mm coin pearls
- 2g 3mm cube beads
- 5 in. (13cm) 22-gauge half-hard wire
- 20 in. (51cm) cable chain, 4mm links
- **2** 7mm jump rings
- Toggle clasp
- Fireline, 6 lb. test
- Beading needles, #10–#12
- Scissors
- Thread conditioner
- Diagonal wire cutters
- Roundnose pliers and chainnose pliers

Stitch up a banner day

Actually, these banners won't even take a whole day to stitch up. Plus, their dimensions can easily be adjusted to fit any design you can imagine. I started with a simple repeating floral pattern and thought of five more potential panels while I stitched it up. I decided to string it on a coordinated bead strand, but a smallish-link chain would also work.

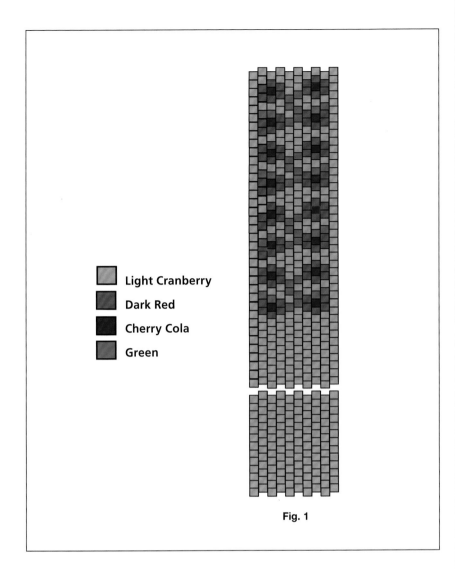

Light Cranberry

Dark Red

Cherry Cola

Green

Fig. 1

Supplies
**Thick ribbon necklace,
17½ in. (44.5cm)**
- 2g 11º cylinder beads, color A
- 1g 11º cylinder beads in each of **3 colors**
- **30** 2.8mm drops
- 3–4mm stop bead
- **2** 7mm jump rings
- Lobster claw clasp
- Beading thread
- Beading needles, #10–#12
- Thread conditioner
- Roundnose pliers and chainnose pliers
- Diagonal wire cutters

Color Guide
11º cylinder beads: Duracoat galvanized matte light cranberry, matte metallic dark red, matte transparent cherry cola, and green Delicas
2.8mm drops: mauve/mocha

Thick ribbon necklace

1. Thread a needle on one end of 36 in. (.9m) of conditioned beading thread. Attach a stop bead about 10 in. (25cm) from one end (Basics, p. 104). Pick up ten 11º cylinder beads following the pattern shown **(fig. 1)**.

2. Work in peyote stitch (Basics, p. 105): Pick up an 11º. Skip the last bead picked up and sew through the next bead in the row.

3. Pick up another 11º, skip a bead, and sew through the next bead. Continue until your thread is exiting the last bead in the row.

4. Start each new row by picking up an 11º, skipping and passing through the first raised bead, which will be the last bead added in the previous row.

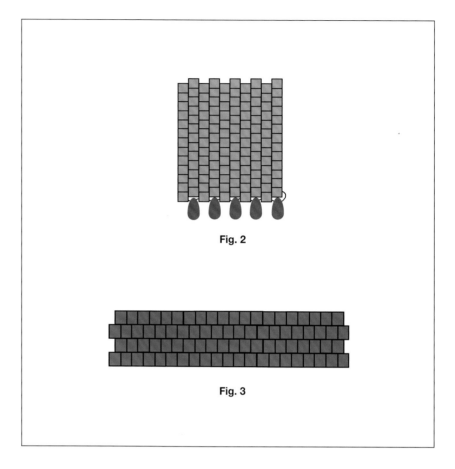

Fig. 2

Fig. 3

TIP

I decided to leave the segment of the banner after the fold just one color, but you can change your pattern throughout the project or stitch a new contrasting pattern for the back portion.

5. Following the pattern, stitch four sets of flowers, then stitch only color A 11ºs until the banner is the desired length. Mine is 4½ in. (11.4cm).

6. Remove the stop bead and thread the needle on the tail. Stitch drop beads into the gaps in the peyote. Weave the thread back through the beadwork and trim the thread **(fig. 2)**.

7. Following steps 1–4, make the narrow band that will secure the banner. You'll only need 12 in. (30cm) of thread for the band. It's 20 rows of four beads **(fig. 3)**.

8. To string the necklace, cut a 23-in. (58cm) piece of flexible beading wire and string 17 in. (43cm) of an alternating pattern of 11ºs and drops. I made the accent color in the banner, the dominant color in the strand.

9. On one end, string a crimp bead, a cylinder bead, and a lobster claw clasp. Go back through the beads just strung and tighten the wire.

Crimp the crimp bead (Basics, p. 103) and trim the excess wire. Repeat on the opposite end, substituting a soldered jump ring for the clasp.

10. Fold the banner over the strand (or chain), and secure it with the narrow band. Wrap the band around the banner and zip up the edges in the back (Basics, p. 106). For extra security, you can tack the band to the back of the banner with the excess thread, hiding the knot in the beads.

...triple your banners!

Thin ribbon pattern

TIP

As with the other peyote projects, I used my Quick Start cards for the banner and the band (see p. 23).

Three-ribbon necklace

Make three ribbons following the thin ribbon pattern on this page. Instead of folding each ribbon, string the top 11º seed beads onto a piece of black artistic wire and string 11ºs between and around the ribbons. Attach the ribbon segment to 9-in. (23cm) segments of chain with wrapped loops (Basics, p. 102) and use a jump ring to attach a lobster claw clasp on one end (Basics, p. 103). Attach another jump ring to the opposite end of the necklace.

Three-ribbon necklace, 20 in. (51cm)

- 1g 11º cylinder beads in each of four colors
- 3–4mm stop bead
- 4 in. (10cm) craft wire, black
- 18 in. (46cm) chain, 8mm links
- **2** 7mm jump rings
- Lobster claw clasp
- Beading thread
- Beading needles, #10–#12
- Thread conditioner

- Roundnose pliers and chainnose pliers
- Diagonal wire cutters

Color Guide

11º cylinder beads: opaque black, opaque white, opaque rainbow orange, and opaque rainbow berry fuchsia Delicas

Delicate details

I love using filigrees in my designs. They're versatile and beautiful on their own, but—more importantly— they offer an elegant or edgy canvas for beads and patinas (or both). The beaded princess-cut components I used in this project look like they could have been unearthed in an antique shop, but they are actually super-quick and easy to put together.

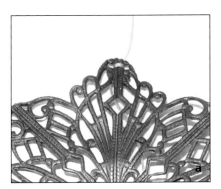

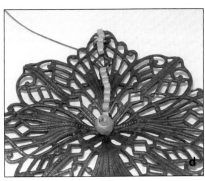

Pendant

1. Cut a 24-in. (61cm) piece of thread. Condition the thread and thread a needle at one end. Use an overhand knot (Basics, p. 104) to tie the end of the thread around the center bar of the segment near the edge of the filigree **(photo a)**.

2. Pick up a color A 11º cylinder bead and position it against the filigree. Bring the thread around the filigree and through the bead again. Add two more As, a color B cylinder bead, and an A the same way **(photo b)**.

3. Wrap the thread two or three times around the edge of the diamond shape and attach an A under the base of the diamond as in step 1. Using ladder stitch (Basics, p. 104), add a B, four As, a B, and an A to the bead attached in step 2 **(photo c)**.

4. Bring the thread up through the center of the filigree. Pick up a 4mm fire-polished bead and an 11º seed bead. Sew back through the fire-polished bead **(photo d)**.

Supplies

Necklace, 18 in. (46cm)
- 56mm princess-cut filigree
- 4mm fire-polished bead
- **4** 8º seed beads
- 11º cylinder beads
  - **56** color A
  - **20** color B
- **5** 11º seed beads
- Premade necklace chain
- Spring-ring clasp
- **4** 7mm soldered jump rings
- Beading thread
- **2** pairs of chainnose pliers
- Diagonal wire cutters
- Beading needles, #10–#12
- Thread conditioner

Color Guide
4mm fire-polished beads:
neon electric purple fire
8º seed beads: plum
11º seed beads: matte
chartreuse
11º cylinder beads: matte
lavender and matte lime
green Delicas
patinas: verdigris and a
combination of moss and clay

TIP

I used Vintaj patinas for a more modern-looking pendant. I also experimented with a two-tone look.

TIP

If you want to hide the thread, use a color that blends into the tone of the filigree. I used a brown tone for this project. On the other hand, a contrasting thread color would add another layer of color to the piece.

5. Move to the next segment to the right to create a row of beads at a 45-degree angle from the first. As in step 1, attach two As next to the center bead. Bring the thread up through the diamond-shaped opening and pick up an 8º seed bead and an 11º seed bead. Sew back through

the 8º. Attach three more As and one B along the column as shown **(photo e)**.

6. Repeat steps 1–5 three more times as you move around the filigree. Tie off the end of the thread with two overhand knots, hidden under the beads. Trim the excess thread (Basics, p. 104). Attach a jump ring to each side of the corner segment.

7. Center the pendant on an 18-in. (46cm) piece of chain. On one end, use a jump ring to attach a spring ring clasp. Attach another jump ring to the opposite end.

...add flair with filigrees!

Earrings

For each earring, follow pendant steps 1–4. Attach a jump ring to each side of the corner segment. Attach both jump rings to the loop of an earring wire.

Earrings

- **2** 56m princess-cut filigrees
- **2** 4mm fire-polished beads
- **8** 8º seed beads
- 11º cylinder beads
  - **20** color A
  - **6** color B
- **2** 11º seed beads
- **4** 7mm soldered jump rings
- Pair of earring wires
- Beading thread
- **2** pairs of chainnose pliers
- Diagonal wire cutters
- Beading needles, #10–#12
- Thread conditioner

Front & center

Some cones, like these embellished brick stitch components, are far too beautiful to be hidden in the back. For these necklaces, I positioned them front and center-ish (I'm a fan of the off-center focal). You can create endless color combinations by nestling cones in descending sizes; use the seam created by the easy-peasy connection as a resting place for small pearls.

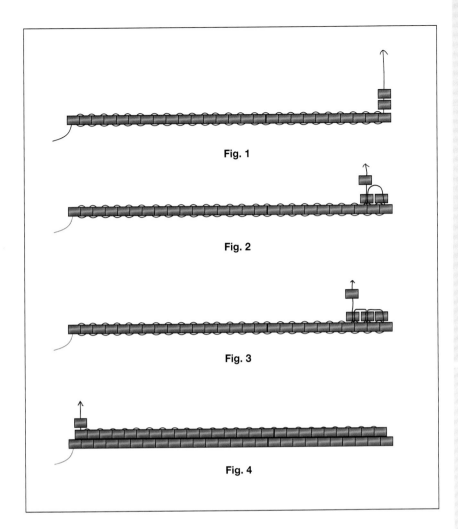

Fig. 1

Fig. 2

Fig. 3

Fig. 4

Supplies

**Triple cone necklace,
21 in. (53cm)**

- **24–26** 14mm round beads
- **8** 12mm pearls
- **31–33** 4mm pearls
- 2g 11º cylinder beads, in each of **3** colors
- Beading thread
- Flexible beading wire, .014
- **2** crimp beads
- Toggle clasp
- Beading needles, #10–#12
- Thread conditioner
- Roundnose pliers and chainnose pliers
- Diagonal wire cutters

Color Guide
11º cylinder beads: matte teal, matte forest green, and Duracoat Columbine
Pearls: vintage gold and mauve

Make the cones

1. Thread a needle on one end of a 24-in. (61cm) piece of conditioned thread. Use 11º cylinder beads to create a 26-bead ladder (Basics, p. 106). This will be the longest row in the cone.

2. For the second row, pick up two cylinders **(fig. 1)**. Skip over the first exposed thread loop and sew through the second loop. Pass back through the second bead and tighten the thread.

3. Pick up an 11º **(fig. 2)**. Sew through the next thread loop and then back up through the cylinder **(fig. 3)**. Continue until the end of the row. This row will have 25 beads.

4. Repeat steps 2 and 3 for each subsequent row. Each row will have one less bead **(fig. 4)**. Add rows until you have 11.

5. To form the cone, bring the sides together and sew down through the top bead on the left side and back up through the top bead on the right. Sew down through two beads on the right side and up through the second bead on the left. Continue like this until you reach the end of the rows. **(fig. 5, p. 58)**. Bring the thread all the way back up one right side and tie the two ends together with a surgeon's knot (Basics, p. 104). Trim the excess thread.

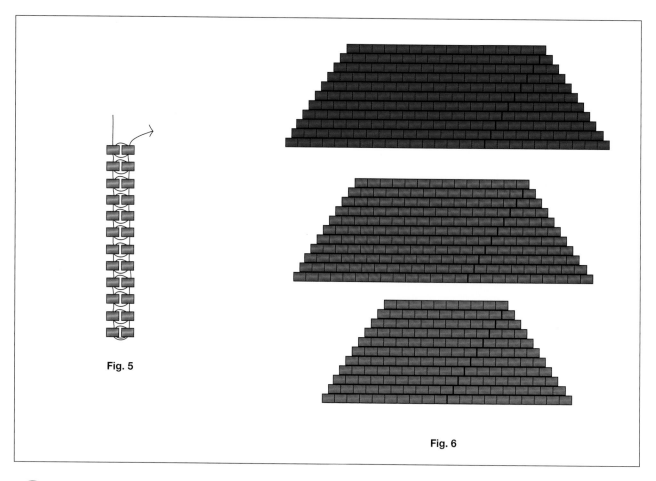

Fig. 5

Fig. 6

 TIP

If you're a symmetry fan, center the pearl and cones and string the same number of beads on each side, skipping the 12mm pearl trio.

6. Make a second cone beginning with a 24-bead ladder and a third with a 20-bead ladder **(fig. 6)**.

7. Nestle the three cones and embellish them with three pearls: Thread a needle on a 12-in. (30cm) piece of conditioned thread. Tie two or three square knots on one end, leaving a 3-in. (7.6cm) tail. Starting from inside the cones, bring the needle up between the third and fourth row of the small cone. Pick up a pearl and bring the thread around the edge of the small cone and up through the third and fourth row of

the middle cone. Pick up a pearl and bring the thread down between the first and second row of the middle cone. Bring the needle up between the third and fourth bead of the largest cone. Pick up a pearl and bring the thread down between the first and second row of the large cone. Tie the end of the thread to the tail with a surgeon's knot (Basics, p. 104) and trim the excess thread.

Finish the necklace

1. Make two nested cones. Cut a 27-in. (69cm) piece of flexible beading wire. String a 12mm pearl. On each end, string a set of cones, narrow end first, and two more pearls.

2. On one end, string an alternating pattern of 10 14mm beads and 10 4mm pearls. On the other end, string an alternating pattern of 14

14mm beads and 13 4mm pearls, but about 4½ in. (11.4cm) from one end, add three 12mm pearls to create a visual balance with the cones. Check the fit, allowing about 1½ in. (3.8cm) for finishing. Add or remove beads as needed.

3. On each end, string a crimp bead, a 4mm pearl, and half of a toggle clasp. Go back through the beads you just strung and tighten the wire. Crimp the crimp bead (Basics, p. 103) and trim the excess wire.

 TIP

To give the cone bail a flattened look, add a little floor polish and press under a book until the polish dries. Wrap the pendant in wax paper to keep it from sticking to the book or table.

...make it simple!

Pendant necklace

1. Follow "Make the cones," steps 1–5, to make a small, unembellished cone; this will act as a bail for a flat charm.

2. Make a plain loop on a 2-in. (5cm) piece of 22-gauge wire. String a 4mm pearl, the cone, and four more pearls. Then make another plain loop. Attach the charm to the bottom loop and use a jump ring to attach the top loop to a chain. String a pearl on a headpin and make a plain loop. Attach the dangle next to the charm on the bottom plain loop.

**Pendant necklace,
30 in. (76cm)**
- 16mm charm
- **6** 4mm pearls
- 2g 11º cylinder beads
- Beading thread
- 2 in. (5cm) 22-gauge wire
- 2-in. headpin
- 21 in. (53cm) ball chain with connecter
- Beading needles, #10–#12
- Thread conditioner

- Roundnose pliers and chainnose pliers
- Diagonal wire cutters

Color Guide
11º cylinder beads: Duracoat Op Columbine

Bicone bands

I've had a strand of dagger beads in my stash
forever. They seemed like such a good idea when I
bought them, but then I was never sure what to do
with them. I wanted to dress them up a bit, but still
maintain a bit of edginess. And so they gathered dust.
These simple right-angle weave bands turned out to be
a great way to spruce up the daggers—either with
a simple band or a whole crystal snuggie.

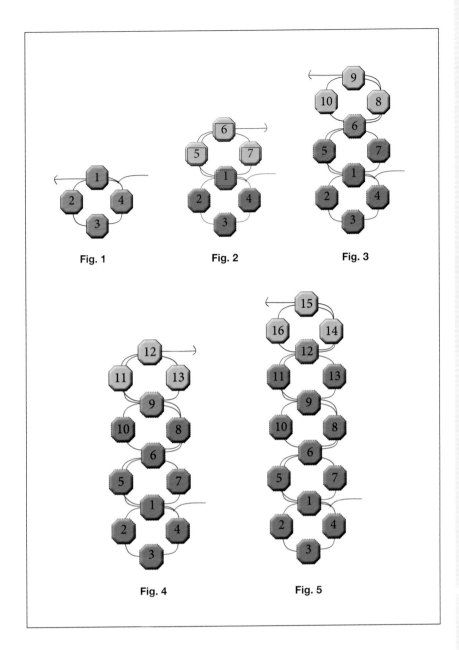

Fig. 1

Fig. 2

Fig. 3

Fig. 4

Fig. 5

Supplies
Multiple dagger necklace, 20 in. (51cm)
- Strand of graduated dagger beads
- **231** 3mm bicones
- 17 in. (43cm) double-link chain, 9mm links
- S-hook clasp
- Flexible beading wire, .014
- Fireline, 6 lb. test
- Beading needles, #10–#12
- **2** pairs of chainnose pliers
- Diagonal wire cutters
- Scissors
- Two-part epoxy

Dagger snuggie necklace, 23 in. (58 cm)
- 40mm dagger bead
- **88** 3mm bicones
- 19 in. (48cm) 1mm leather cord
- **2** 1mm cord ends
- **2** jump rings
- Lobster claw clasp
- Fireline, 6 lb. test
- Beading needles, #10–#12
- **2** pairs of chainnose pliers
- Diagonal wire cutters
- Scissors
- Two-part epoxy

Color Guide
Multiple dagger necklace crystals: jet

Dagger snuggie necklace crystals: Pacific opal

Bicone bands

1. Cut a 24-in. (61cm) piece of Fireline and thread a needle on one end. Pick up four 3mm bicones and sew through the first bicone again. Tie the bicones into a ring with a square knot (Basics, p. 104) **(fig. 1)**.

2. Pick up three bicones (5, 6, and 7). Sew through 1, 5, and 6 again **(fig. 2)**.

3. Pick up three bicones (8, 9, and 10). Sew through 6, 8, and 9 again **(fig. 3)**.

4. Pick up three bicones (11, 12, and 13). Sew through 9, 11, and 12 again **(fig. 4)**.

5. Pick up three bicones (14, 15, and 16). Sew through 12, 14, and 15 again **(fig. 5)**.

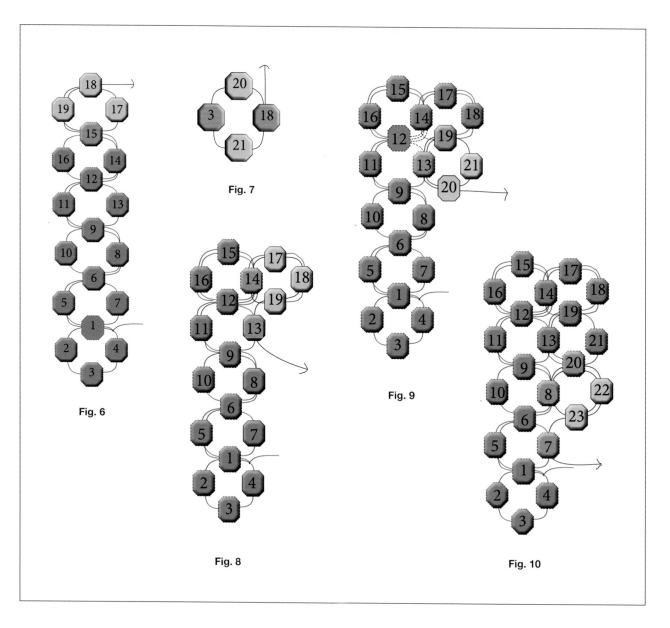

Fig. 6

Fig. 7

Fig. 8

Fig. 9

Fig. 10

6. Pick up three bicones (19, 18, and 17). Sew through 15, 19, and 18 again **(fig. 6)**.

7. Bring the edges together. Exiting bicone 18, pick up a new bicone (20), the bicone from the other end (3), and another new bicone (21). Sew through the circle again. Following the bead path, weave the thread back to the beadwork **(fig. 7)**. Tie an overhand knot (Basics, p. 104), and trim the excess thread to complete the band. Make a total of 11 bands.

Multiple dagger necklace

1. Choose 11 dagger beads from the strand. Pick a long bead for the

center and 10 matching pairs of descending size. Cut a 10-in. (25cm) piece of beading wire. Slide a bicone band on the dagger, positioning the center of two of the bicone circles over the dagger holes. Center the banded dagger on the wire. On each end, string a bicone and one of the next largest pair of daggers (without bands). Continue stringing bicones and daggers of descending size, skipping the bands on every other pair.

2. Set the strand aside and cut two 8-in. (20cm) pieces of chain. On one end of each chain, remove one of the links in the pair. (The chain I used had

unsoldered links, so I could remove one by opening it like a jump ring.) On each end of the dagger strand, string a crimp bead and the single link of each piece of chain. Go back though the last beads strung. Tighten the wire and crimp the crimp bead. Trim the excess wire. On one end of the chain, attach an S-hook clasp.

4. Use two-part epoxy to attach bicone rings to the unbound daggers. Position them so they rest just under the bands that were strung on the beading wire.

Dagger snuggie necklace

1. Follow steps 1–5 of the bicone bands. (Only sew through bead 14 in step 5.) For a second column, pick up three bicones (17, 18, and 19). Sew through 14, 17, 18, 19, and 13 **(fig. 8)**.

2. Pick up two bicones (20 and 21). Sew through 19, 13, and 20 **(fig. 9)**.

3. Pick up two bicones (22 and 23). Sew through 8, 20, 22, 23, and 7 **(fig. 10)**.

4. Pick up two bicones (24 and 25). Sew through 23, 7, and 4 **(fig. 11)**.

5. Pick up two bicones (26 and 27). Sew through 24, 4, 26, and 27 **(fig. 12)**. Add five more columns. Start each column by picking up three bicones and then adding two for each of the remaining ring in the column.

6. Create a tube by adding six more bicones to link the two sides **(fig. 13)**. Exit bicone 82 and add bicone 83. Sew through bicone 16 and add bicone 84. Sew through bicones 82, 83, 16, 84, and 79. Pick up bicone 85 and sew through bicone 10. Pick up bicone 86 and sew through bicones 78, 85, 10, 86, and 75. Pick up bicone 87 and sew through bicones 5, 86, 75, 87, and 2. Pick up bicone 88 and sew through bicones 73, 87, 2, and 88.

7. To assemble the necklace, cut a 19-in. (48cm) piece of leather cord. Center a 40mm dagger. Close cord ends over the ends of the cord with chainnose pliers. Use a jump ring to attach a lobster claw clasp. Attach another jump ring to the other end. Use two-part epoxy to secure the bicone snuggie around the dagger 4–5mm below the cord.

Dagger snuggie necklace

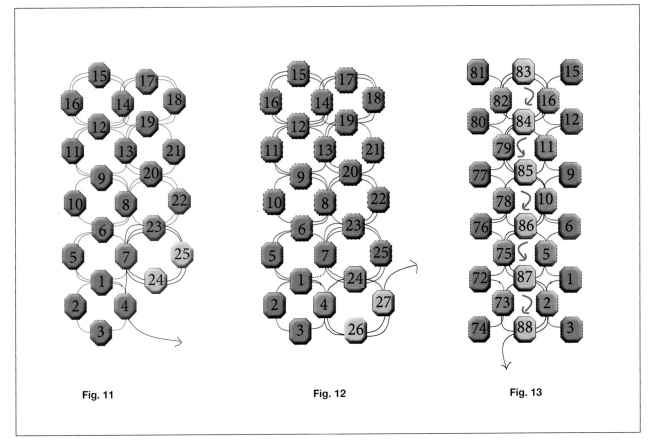

Fig. 11   Fig. 12   Fig. 13

...build a pair of earrings!

Earrings

For each earring, make a bicone band, following steps 1–7 of "Bicone bands." Slide a bicone band on a dagger, positioning the center of two of the bicone circles over the dagger holes. Cut a 2-in. (5cm) piece of 24-gauge artistic wire. Center the banded dagger on the wire and make a set of wraps above the bead (Basics, p. 103). Attach the dangle to an earring wire with a wrapped loop (Basics, p. 102).

Earrings

- **2** 12mm dagger beads
- **42** 3mm bicones
- Fireline, 6 lb. test
- 4 in. (10cm) 24-gauge wire
- Pair of earring wires
- Beading needles, #10–#12
- Roundnose pliers and chainnose pliers
- Diagonal wire cutters
- Scissors

Tiny tapestries

Using simple square stitch to create a series of tiny tapestries, you can create your own personal art gallery. String a line of rectangles or use interlocking shapes to add even more interest. I used subtle color combinations to make the stitched flags less "flaggy," but bolder color choices will create an eye-catching, graphic look.

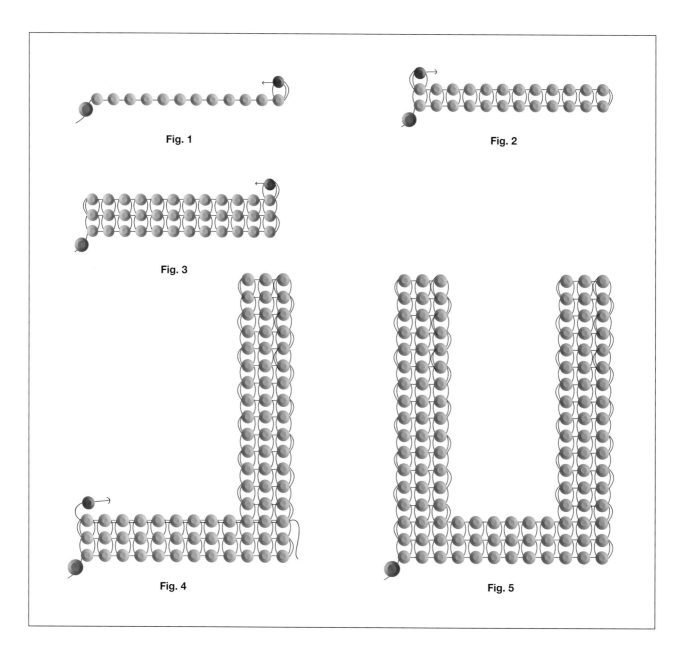

Fig. 1

Fig. 2

Fig. 3

Fig. 4

Fig. 5

Follow square-stitch patterns

1. Thread a needle at one end of a 36-in. (.9m) piece of conditioned thread. Attach a stop bead about 6 in. (15cm) from the end (Basics, p. 104). Following the color pattern for the u-shaped flag (see patterns, next page), pick up the 12 11º cylinder beads from the first row (from left to right). Pick up the first 11º from the second row (you'll start the second row on the right). Bring the thread through the last 11º in the first row and back through the first 11º in the second row **(fig. 1)**.

2. Pick up the next 11º in the second row. Bring the thread through the 11º below it and back through the 11º just picked up, and continue with the third 11º in the row (and so on) **(fig. 2)**. Repeat for a third row **(fig. 3)**.

3. Stitch a three-bead fourth row. Continue stitching three-bead rows on one side until you have a total of 14. Weave the end of the thread back through a few stitches, always following the original thread path. Trim the thread.

4. Thread a needle at one end of a 18-in. (46cm) piece of conditioned thread. From the right, bring the thread through the third 12-bead row, leaving a 6-in. (15cm) tail. Pick up the next 11º **(fig. 4)**. Stitch 14 three-bead rows to finish the U **(fig. 5)**. Remove the stop bead. One by one, thread the needle to the end of the thread tails and weave back through a few stitches, always following the original thread path. Trim the threads.

5. Following the color patterns, stitch two thin flags and both wide flags (left and right), using a 24-in. (61cm) piece of beading thread for each.

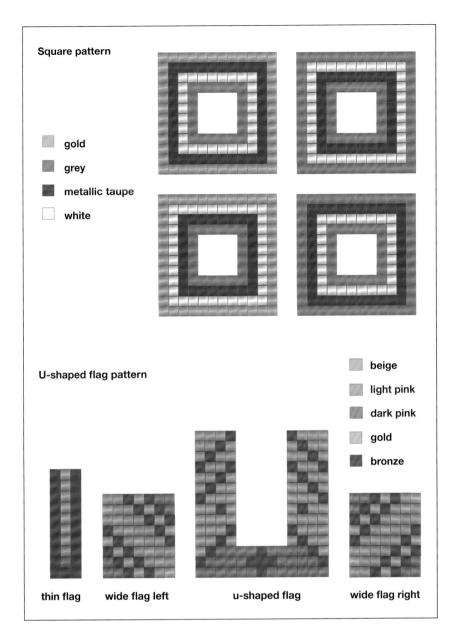

Square pattern

gold

grey

metallic taupe

white

U-shaped flag pattern

beige

light pink

dark pink

gold

bronze

thin flag   wide flag left   u-shaped flag   wide flag right

Supplies

Bracelet, 7½ in. (19cm)

- **8** 12m rondelles
- **7** 6mm round beads
- **3g** 11º cylinder beads, in each of four colors
- **2** crimp beads
- Toggle clasp
- Beading thread
- Scissors
- Flexible beading wire, .014
- Beading needles, #10–#12
- Thread conditioner
- 6 in. (15cm) 24-gauge wire
- Diagonal wire cutters
- Crimping pliers

Necklace, 17 in. (43 cm)

- **3g** 11º cylinder beads, in each of five colors
- **2** crimp beads
- Lobster claw clasp
- 7mm soldered jump ring
- Beading thread
- Scissors
- Flexible beading wire, .014
- Beading needles, #10–#12
- Thread conditioner
- Diagonal wire cutters
- Crimping pliers

Color Guide

Necklace and earrings

11º cylinder beads: copper-plated, Duracoat galvanized metallic gold, luminous sea coral, matte Op red AB, and Op light peach Ceylon Delicas

Bracelet

11º cylinder beads: opaque steel grey, opaque matte white, Duracoat galvanized metallic gold, and copper-plated Delicas

Bracelet

1. Turn the U-shaped flags into square bead frames: Stitch four 12-bead rows for the bottom. Stitch five four-bead rows on one side, then follow the thread (along the existing thread path) to the opposite end of the fourth 12-bead row. Stitch five four-bead rows on that side and then pick up four beads and the top four-bead row on the first side. To finish, stitch three more 12-bead rows across the top. Make seven frames.

2. On a 13-in. (33cm) piece of beading wire, string a crimp bead and half of the clasp. Go back through the crimp bead, and crimp (Basics, p. 103). String a 12mm rondelle, one side of a frame, a 6mm round bead, and the other side of the frame. Repeat until you reach the end. Then crimp the other half of the clasp to the opposite end of the bracelet.

TIP

In making the U-shaped flag, I added a new thread when adding the fourth side because it was impossible to follow the thread path back to where I needed it to be. If you don't want to add the second thread, make the flag either one row taller or shorter. Adjust the other flags accordingly.

Necklace

1. Cut a 23-in. (58cm) piece of beading wire. On the wire, center one side of the U, an 11º cylinder bead, a thin flag, an 11º, and the other side of the U.

2. On each end, string an 11º, a thick flag, an 11º, and a thin flag. String 11ºs in a random color pattern until the necklace is within ½ in. (1.3cm) of the finished length. Check the fit,

allowing ½ in. for finishing, and add or remove beads as necessary.

3. On one end, string a crimp bead, an 11º, and a lobster claw clasp. Go back through the beads just strung and tighten the wire. Crimp the crimp bead (Basics, p. 103) and trim the excess wire. Repeat on the opposite end, substituting a soldered jump ring for the clasp.

...make long, elegant earrings!

If you plan to use floor polish to further stiffen your beadwork as I did in the bracelet and earrings (but not the necklace), string a piece of 24-gauge wire through the holes you plan to string the beading wire through before you add the polish. Otherwise, the hardened polish will block the holes. Another option is to CAREFULLY add the polish after the bracelet has been strung.

Earrings

Stitch two thin flags. For each earring, cut a 3-in. (7.6cm) piece of 24-gauge wire. Center a flag on the wire and make a set of wraps above the flag (Basics, p. 103). Attach the dangle to an earring wire.

Earrings

- 1g each 11º cylinder beads in four colors
- 6 in. (15cm) 24-gauge wire
- Beading thread
- Beading needles, #10–#12
- Scissors
- Thread conditioner
- Pair of earring wires
- Diagonal wire cutters
- Roundnose pliers and chainnose pliers

A stylish, tile-ish look

The invention of Tila beads paved the way for a revolution in beadweaving, spawning an ever-growing list of new shapes. If you're looking to try them for the first time or add a quick project to your existing Tila repertoire, this tennis bracelet is perfect.

Supplies

Bracelet, 7½ in. (19cm)

- **36–42** Tila beads
- **19–22** 3x5mm Rulla beads
- 1g 8º seed beads
- 1g 11º seed beads
- 1–2-in. (2.5–5cm) extender chain
- **2** 7mm jump rings
- Lobster claw clasp
- Beading thread
- Beading needles, #10–#12
- Scissors
- Thread conditioner
- Diagonal wire cutters
- **2** pairs of chainnose pliers

Color Guide
Bracelet
Tila beads: opaque matte violet blue luster
Rulla beads: opaque amethyst luster
11º seed beads: matte polaris permanent galvanized
8º seed beads: silver-lined matte purple

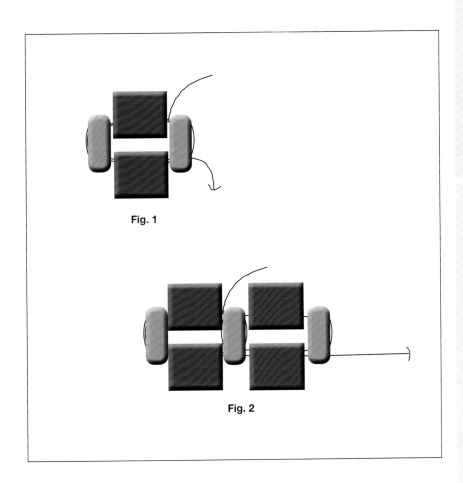

Fig. 1

Fig. 2

Bracelet

1. Thread a needle on a 36-in. (.9m) piece of conditioned beading thread. Pick up a Tila bead, one hole of a Rulla bead, the other hole of a Rulla, a Tila, one hole of a Rulla, and the other hole of a Rulla. (You will only use one hole of the Tila for this section.) Tie the ends together with two overhand knots (Basics, p. 104), leaving a 3-in. (7.6cm) tail.

Sew through the first Tila, both holes of the first Rulla, the second Tila, and one hole of the second Rulla. Tighten the thread **(fig. 1)**.

2. Pick up a Tila, both holes of a Rulla, a Tila, and both holes of the second Rulla from step 1. Sew through the first Tila from this step again and one hole of the new Rulla, and tighten the thread **(fig. 2)**.

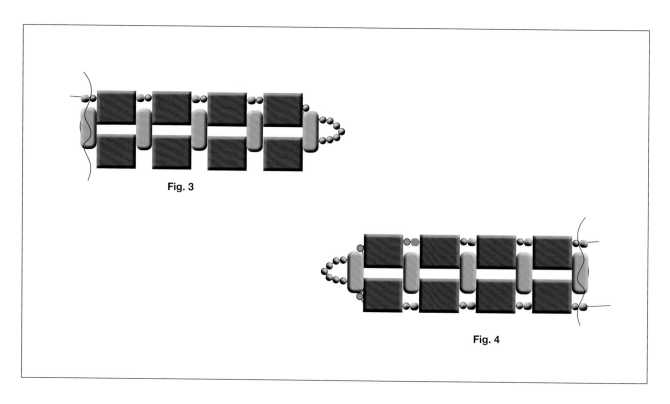

Fig. 3

Fig. 4

3. Repeat step 2 until the bracelet is within 1 in. (2.5cm) of the finished length. Pick up seven 11º seed beads and sew through the second hole of the last Rulla added.

4. Now you will use the open holes in the Tilas: Pick up an 11º seed bead and sew through the open hole of the next Tila. Pick up an 11º, an 8º seed bead, and the next Tila. Continue adding an 11º and an 8º between each Tila until you reach the end of the bracelet **(fig. 3)**.

4. Finish this end of the bracelet the same way as the first: Pick up an 11º and sew through the first hole of a Rulla. Pick up seven 11ºs and sew through the second hole of the Rulla. Pick up an 11º and sew through the second hole of the adjacent Tila. Add an 11º and an 8º between each Tila on the second side as in step 4 **(fig. 4)**. Tie an overhand knot after the last Tila (Basics, p. 104) and trim the excess thread.

5. On one end, open a jump ring (Basics, p. 103) and attach a lobster claw clasp to the seed bead loop. Repeat on the opposite end, substituting the extender chain for the clasp.

...add a twist with chain!

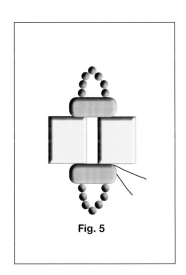

Fig. 5

TIP

Even with the tightest wire, the earring Tilas were a little floppy. I tried to rework the design, but always liked the original arrangement best, so I added the tiniest bit of glue between the bottom Rulla and the Tilas to hold them in place.

Earrings

1. For each earring, thread a needle on a 12-in. (30cm) piece of conditioned beading thread. Pick up a Tila, one hole of a Rulla, six or seven 11º seed beads, the other hole of the Rulla, a new Tila, one hole of a new Rulla, six or seven 11ºs, and the other hole of the last Rulla. Sew through all of the beads again, tighten the thread, and tie two overhand knots (Basics, p. 104) **(fig. 5)**.

2. To add the chain, string a headpin down through the outer hole of each Tila. Make a plain loop (Basics, p. 102) on each headpin. On each loop, attach one end of a 1-in. (2.5cm) chain **(photo)**.

Earrings
- **4** Tila beads
- **4** 3x5mm Rulla beads
- **24–28** 11º seed beads
- 2 in. (5cm) of 3mm-link chain
- **2** 2-in. (5cm) headpins
- Pair of earring wires
- Beading thread
- Beading needles, #10–#12
- Scissors
- Thread conditioner
- Diagonal wire cutters
- Chainnose pliers and roundnose pliers
- E6000 adhesive (optional)

Color Guide
Tila beads: opaque matte cream
Rulla beads: Apollo amethyst
11º seed beads: metallic gold

Ombre reef

Inspiration sometimes comes in unexpected ways. A picture of Katy Perry's hair sparked an idea for this ombre "coral" necklace. You can adjust the number of coral branches to make the necklace as fluffy as you want it. Whip up two more and you have a pair of lightweight earrings. I think Katy would approve!

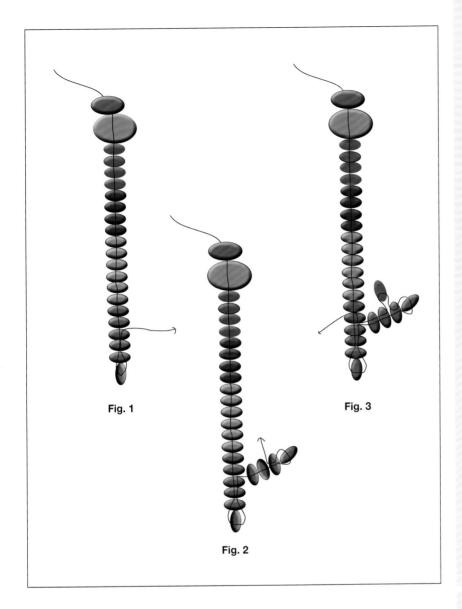

Fig. 1

Fig. 2

Fig. 3

Make a coral branch

1. Cut an 18-in. (46cm) piece of beading thread, thread a needle on one end, and attach a stop bead, leaving a 3-in. (7.6cm) tail (Basics, p. 104). Pick up a 4mm rondelle, four color A 11º seed beads, four color B 11º seed beads, and six each of colors C and D 11º seed beads. Skipping the last bead picked up, sew back through the previous three beads **(fig. 1)**.

2. Pick up four Ds. Skip the last bead picked up and sew back through the next bead **(fig. 2)**. Tighten the thread.

3. Pick up an A. Sew back through the remaining Ds and the next bead on the main branch. Tighten the thread **(fig. 3)**.

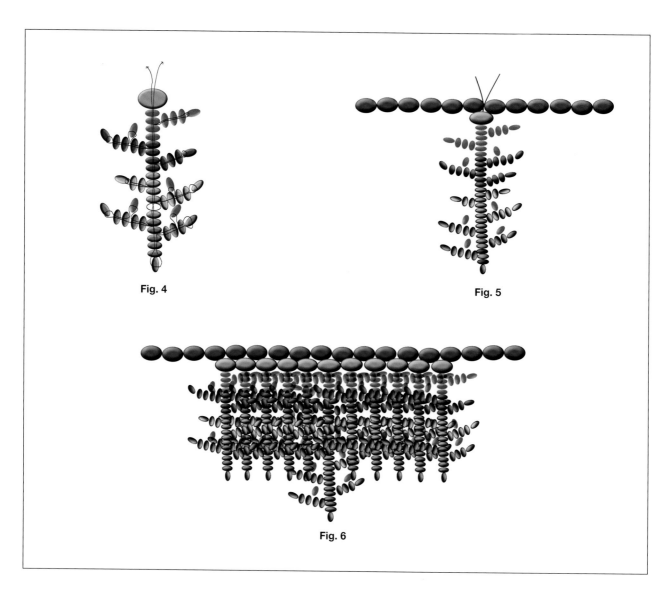

Fig. 4

Fig. 5

Fig. 6

4. Following the path in the illustration, add more branches **(fig. 4)**. Always make the side branches the same color as the segment of the main branch they are emerging from. Remove the stop bead and set aside. Make a total of 20 coral units with a 20-bead main branch. Make one longer coral unit by adding two more beads to each color segment and adding four or five more side branches.

Necklace

1. Cut a 23-in. (58cm) piece of flexible beading wire and center 22 round beads. On each side, string rondelles interspersed with rounds until the strand is within 1 in. (2.5cm) of the finished length. Check the fit, allowing about 1 in. for finishing. Add or remove beads as necessary. Attach a piece of tape or a bead stopper to each end.

2. Center the longest coral unit on the strand. Tie the Fireline ends around the flexible beading wire with two overhand knots (Basics, p. 104) **(fig. 5)**. Trim the excess thread, hiding the knot between the beads. On each side, tie on 10 coral units between the beads **(fig. 6)**.

3. On one end, string a crimp bead, a rondelle, and half of the toggle clasp. Go back through the beads just strung and tighten the wire. Crimp the crimp bead (Basics, p. 103) and trim the excess wire. Repeat on the opposite end with the other half of the clasp.

...make an understated accessory!

Another idea

I made a less fluffy version of the necklace with just seven coral units and attached them to a strand of Labradorite pebbles. I made the longer center unit in all black beads and added one coral unit in each blue on either side, creating a horizontal ombre effect.

Earrings

For each earring, make a coral unit. Tie the unit to the loop of an earring wire using an overhand knot (Basics, p. 104). Bring the ends of the Fireline back though four or five beads of the main branch and trim the excess thread.

Beaded greenery

I picked up these wood barrels on impulse while buying some Halloween decorations at the craft store. I must have already been missing the summer greenery, because my first thought was to add some verdant accents. I limited the accents to just one bead, so it would really pop. Beaded right-angle-weave (RAW) outfits for a whole strand would be a lush statement.

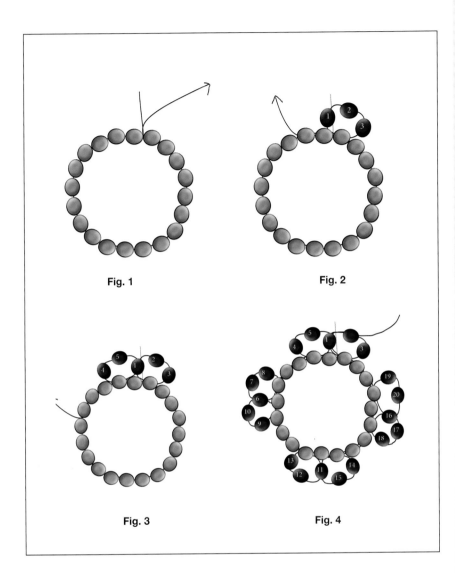

Fig. 1

Fig. 2

Fig. 3

Fig. 4

Supplies

Necklace, 19 in. (48cm)

- **16–18** 18–22mm wood barrel beads
- **5** 8mm rondelles
- **12–14** 5mm round beads
- **1g** 11º seed beads in colors A and B
- **1g** 15º Charlottes
- **2** crimp beads
- Toggle clasp
- Flexible beading wire, .014
- Beading thread
- Beading needles, #10–#12
- Scissors
- Thread conditioner
- Chainnose pliers or crimping pliers
- Diagonal wire cutters

Color Guide

8mm rondelles: celadon green
11º seed beads: opaque forest green and opaque lime green
15º Charlottes: bronze

Embellishing the necklace bead

1. Thread a needle on one end of a 36-in. (.9m) piece of conditioned beading thread. Pick up 20 color A 11º seed beads. Tie an overhand knot (Basics, p. 104) **(fig. 1)**.

2. Pick up three color B 11º seed beads and sew back through the A just exited and the two adjacent As **(fig. 2)**.

3. Pick up two more Bs and sew through the first B picked up in the last step. Sew back through the A just exited in this step and three adjacent As **(fig. 3)**.

4. Repeat steps 2 and 3 three times. Sew through the beadwork to exit a center bead on the edge **(fig. 4)**.

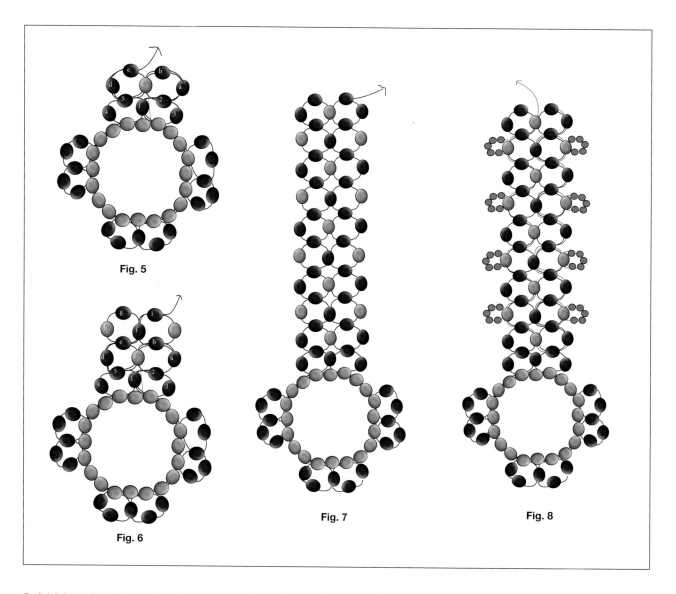

Fig. 5

Fig. 6

Fig. 7

Fig. 8

5. Add three Bs (a, b, c). Sew through 2, a, b, c, and 5. Tighten the thread. Pick up two Bs (d, e). Sew through c, 5, d, and e. Tighten the thread **(fig. 5)**.

6. Pick up two Bs and one A (f, g, h). Sew through e and f. Pick up one B and one A (i and j). Sew through b, f, and i. Tighten the thread **(fig. 6)**.

7. Repeat steps 5 and 6 until you have enough RAW rows to reach the other end of the bead you want to embellish. For these barrel beads, it took 10 rows **(fig. 7)**.

8. Following the red bead path shown, add a five-Charlotte embellishment to all the color A edge beads **(fig. 8)**.

9. Repeat steps 5–8 to finish the remaining columns. Position the ring around one end of the wood bead and wrap the columns around the bead lengthwise. Create a ring on the other end of the bead by picking up a color A bead on each side and between each end bead. Cinch up the columns and sew through the new ring again. Tie an overhand knot (Basics, p. 104).

WHAT IS A CHARLOTTE?

A Charlotte bead is a round bead that has a single facet to produce more shine. Charlotte cuts are most often available as size 13º, but 11º, 8º, and 15º can be found too. Technically, only a 13º is a true Charlotte; the others should be called a "true cut," but it's easier to shop for them as "Charlottes." It is rumored that in 1847, the bead's inventor named it after his daughter.

Necklace

1. Cut a 25-in. (64cm) piece of flexible beading wire. String the embellished barrel bead. On one end, string an alternating pattern of six barrels and six 5mm round beads. On the other end, string an alternating pattern of nine barrels, but instead of just alternating them with the round beads, substitute three rondelles after the first three barrels.

2. Check the fit, allowing 2 in. (5cm) for finishing. Add or remove beads as necessary. Attach a jump ring (Basics, p. 103) to each half of a toggle clasp. On both ends, string a rondelle, a crimp bead, and half of the clasp. Go back through the beads just strung and tighten the wire. Crimp the crimp bead (Basics, p. 103) and trim the excess wire.

...add a little sparkle!

Earrings

Simplify and adjust the same design to cradle two 12mm druzy beads for earrings: Use one type of seed bead for the whole pattern to replicate the druzy look on two of the beads on the strand that lacked the natural detail. String the embellished bead on a headpin between two similarly colored fire-polished beads and make a wrapped loop (Basics, p. 102).

Earrings
- **2** 12mm round druzy agate beads
- **4** 4mm fire-polished round beads
- 1g 11º seed beads
- Beading thread
- **2** 3-in. (7.6cm) headpins
- Pair of earring wires
- Beading needles, #10–#12
- Scissors
- Thread conditioner
- Roundnose pliers and chainnose pliers
- Diagonal wire cutters

Color Guide
15º seed beads: bronze
teal-lined crystal AB

It's OK to bail

A quick piece of square stitch is the base for this versatile bail. The extra effort of making your own finding not only lets you customize your necklace, but gives the potential of heightened glamour to beads that would otherwise spend their lives in a boring, single-file line.

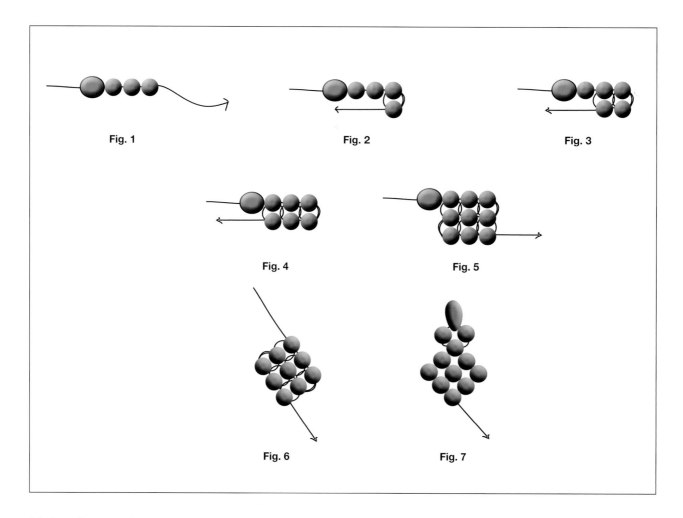

Fig. 1

Fig. 2

Fig. 3

Fig. 4

Fig. 5

Fig. 6

Fig. 7

Make the pendant

1. Thread a needle on one end of a 12-in. (30cm) piece of conditioned thread. Attach a stop bead about 4 in. (15cm) from the end (Basics, p. 104). Pick up three 11º seed beads **(fig. 1)**. Pick up the first 11º for the second row (you'll start the second row on the right). Bring the thread through the last bead in the first row and back through the first bead in the second row **(fig. 2)**.

2. Pick up the next 11º in the second row. Bring the thread through the bead above it and back through the bead just picked up **(fig. 3)**. Continue with the third bead in the row **(fig. 4)**. Repeat for a third row **(fig. 5)**.

3. Remove the stop bead and tilt the square so it hangs as a diamond **(fig. 6)**. On the top thread, pick up an 11º, a drop bead, and an 11º. Sew back through the 11º first exited. Sew through the circle again and work the thread through a couple of beads in

the diamond. Tie an overhand knot (Basics, p. 104) between two beads and trim the excess thread **(fig. 7)**.

4. On the remaining thread, pick up a 16mm nugget and three 11ºs **(fig. 8)**. Bring the thread back up through the nugget and tie an overhand knot. Trim the excess thread **(fig. 9)**. Make 11 pendants.

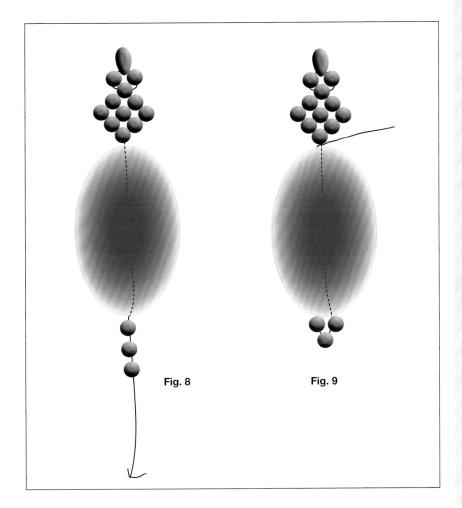

Fig. 8

Fig. 9

Supplies
**Multi-pendant necklace,
16 in. (41cm)**
- **11–13** 16mm quartz nuggets
- 3g 11º seed beads
- 3g drop beads
- **2** crimp beads
- Toggle clasp
- Beading thread
- Flexible beading wire, .014
- Beading needles, #10–#12
- Roundnose pliers and chainnose pliers
- Scissors
- Diagonal wire cutters
- Thread conditioner

Earrings
- **2** pear-shaped top-drilled gemstones
- **18** 8º cylinder beads
- **26** 11º cylinder beads
- Beading thread
- Beading needles, #10–#12
- Thread conditioner
- Scissors
- Pair of earring wires
- **2** pairs of chainnose pliers

Color Guide
Multi-pendant necklace
drop beads: metallic gold
8º seed beads: metallic gold
11º seed beads: transparent gold

Earrings
11º seed beads: semi-matte transparent midnight teal
8º cylinder beads: transparent rainbow matte aqua/lime Delicas

Multi-pendant necklace

1. Cut two 22-in. (56cm) pieces of beading wire. On one wire, center: three 11ºs, a drop, three 11ºs, a pendant, three 11ºs, a drop, and three 11ºs. On each side, string a pendant, three 11ºs, a drop, and three 11ºs. Repeat the sequence on each side. Then, on each side, string a drop and three 11ºs twice. Set aside.

2. On the second piece of beading wire, center three 11ºs, a drop, and three 11ºs. One each side, string an alternating pattern of three pendants and three 11ºs/drop/three 11ºs sequences. Then on each side, string five sequences of one drop/three 11ºs.

3. Bring the strands together. On each side, over both strands, string one drop/three 11ºs sequences until the necklace is within ½ in. (1.3cm) of the desired finished length.

4. On one end, string two or three 8º seed beads, a crimp bead, and half the toggle clasp. Go back through the beads just strung and tighten the wires. Check the length and make sure there are no gaps in the beads where the strands meet. Crimp the crimp bead (Basics, p. 103) and trim the excess wires. Repeat on the other end.

Earrings

1. For each earring, use 8º cylinder beads to make a square stitch diamond, following steps 1 and 2 from "Make the pendant." With the top thread, remove the stop bead, thread a needle, pick up seven 11º cylinders, and sew back through the 11º first exited. Sew through the circle again and work the thread through a couple of beads in the diamond. Tie an overhand knot (Basics, p. 104) between two beads and trim the excess thread.

2. On the remaining thread end, pick up three 11º's, the pear-shaped bead, and four 11º's. Sew through the circle again and work the thread through a couple of beads in the diamond. Tie an overhand knot between two beads and trim the excess thread. Attach the dangle to the loop of an earring wire.

ANOTHER IDEA

Tiny bails could be the answer to those irresistible briolettes with miniscule holes that defy simple stringing. A two- or three-square bail of 15º's could finally get those gems out of the drawer.

...make a delicate drop!

Single-pendant necklace

Make one pendant and center it on a 23-in. (58cm) piece of beading wire. On each side, string an alternating pattern of four 11º cylinder beads and four 8º seed beads. Continue to string 8ºs on each side (I interspersed some 11º seed beads halfway up each side) until the necklace is within ½ in. (1.3cm) of the finished length. On each end, string a crimp bead, an 8º, and half of the toggle clasp. Go back through the beads just strung and tighten the wires. Check the length and add or remove beads as necessary. Crimp the crimp bead (Basics, p. 103) and trim the excess wires. Repeat on the opposite end.

Single-pendant necklace, 17 in. (43cm)

- 16mm quartz nugget
- 2g 8º seed beads
- Approximately **30** 11º seed beads in two colors
- **8** 11º cylinder beads
- **2** crimp beads
- Toggle clasp
- Beading thread
- Beading needles, #10–#12
- Scissors
- Roundnose pliers and chainnose pliers
- Diagonal wire cutters
- Thread conditioner

Color Guide

8º seed beads: metallic gold
11º seed beads: transparent gold and semi-matte transparent midnight teal

Triangle trios

One embellished trio of round beads can be the focal point for a simple necklace—or a sprinkling of them can be a sparkling accent to round-linked chain. They take no time at all, so make both options and layer them! I used milky glass beads, but this can also be a perfect project for pearls. PS: The tiny versions I designed for the earrings would also make great charms for bangle bracelets.

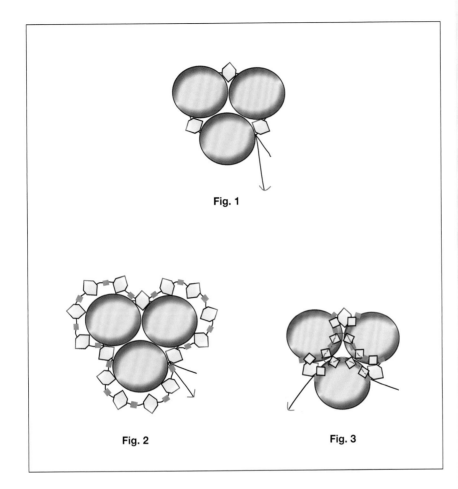

Fig. 1

Fig. 2

Fig. 3

Supplies

Pendant necklace, 24 in. (61cm)

- **3** 15mm round beads
- **15** 4mm bicone crystals
- **15** 11º cylinder beads
- Chain with clasp
- Triangular jump ring
- Beading thread
- Scissors
- Beading needles, #10–#12
- Thread conditioner
- Roundnose pliers and chainnose pliers
- Diagonal wire cutters

Chain necklace, 19 in. (48cm)

- **15** 15mm round beads
- **75** 4mm bicone crystals
- 1g 11º cylinder beads
- 19 in. (48cm) round-link chain, 10mm links
- 15 in. (38cm) 24-gauge wire
- **2** 7mm jump rings
- Toggle clasp
- Beading thread
- Beading needles, #10–#12
- Scissors
- Thread conditioner
- Roundnose pliers and chainnose pliers
- Diagonal wire cutters

Color Guide

Chain necklace

4mm bicones: jet
11º cylinder beads: rainbow medium blueberry/wine Delicas

Pendant necklace

4mm bicones: crystal
11º cylinder beads: matte metallic dark sage green Delicas

Triangle components

1. Thread a needle on one end of an 18-in. (46cm) piece of conditioned thread. Pick up an alternating pattern of three 15mm round beads and three 4mm bicones. Tie them together with two overhand knots (Basics, p. 104) so the round beads form a triangle **(fig. 1)**. Exit a bicone.

2. Pick up an alternating pattern of five 11º cylinder beads and four bicone crystals, and sew through the adjacent bicone in the triangle. Repeat two more times **(fig. 2)**. Move the beads toward the center of the triangle and tighten the thread.

3. On the closest bicone/11º strand, sew back through: an 11º, bicone, an 11º, a bicone, an 11º, and a bicone. Sew through the center bicone-11º-bicone segments on the remaining two strands. Tighten the thread to make a triangle. Sew through the triangle again to snug up the beads. Follow the thread path back to the location of the original overhand knots. Tie another over-hand knot between the original knots and the bicone. Bring the thread through the round bead to the left of the knots, hiding them inside the round as much as possible. Trim the excess thread **(fig. 3)**.

Pendant and chain necklaces

When assembling the necklaces, there are two ways to attach the focal trios.

For the pendant necklace, simply insert a jump ring between two of the 15mm round beads. For the chain necklace, insert a short piece (3 in./7.6cm) of 24-gauge wire through one of the 15mm beads in each trio and make the first half of a wrapped loop on each side (Basics, p. 102). I attached three-link segments of chain between the trios and 6 in. (15cm) of chain on either end. Finish by using a jump ring to attach a clasp half on each end (Basics, p. 103).

PLAY WITH SHAPES

I experimented with wrapping wire above the focals, but while the wraps echoed the triangle theme nicely, I thought they distracted from the beads in these designs.

...a little charm goes a long way!

Earrings

To shrink the design down to earring size, use 5mm round beads and segments of seven 11º cylinder beads. Attach each dangle to the loop of an earring wire.

Earrings

- **6** 5mm round beads
- **42** 11º cylinder beads
- Pair of earring wires
- Beading thread
- Beading needles, #10–#12
- Thread conditioner
- Roundnose pliers and chainnose pliers
- Diagonal wire cutters

Color Guide

11º cylinder beads: rainbow medium blueberry/wine Delicas

Herringbone flair

This project should really be called "Letting it go." I had the structure of what I wanted the flared herringbone spacers to look like in my head, but I initially wanted to use them with mermaid beads. I decided I needed to include some other colors in the spacers. A half-dozen color experiments later, I finally concluded the richly detailed beads did not need any help to shine.

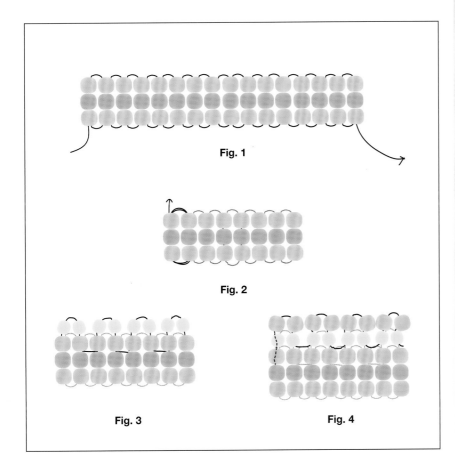

Fig. 1

Fig. 2

Fig. 3

Fig. 4

Supplies

Necklace, 21 in. (53cm)

- **5** 20mm pearls
- **1g** each 11º round seed beads or cylinder beads in three colors
- **9 in. (23cm)** 22-gauge wire
- **16 in. (41cm)** large-link chain
- **2** 7mm jump rings
- Lobster-claw clasp
- Beading thread
- Beading needles, #10–#12
- Scissors
- Thread conditioner
- Roundnose pliers and chainnose pliers
- Diagonal wire cutters

Color Guide

Necklace

11º round seed beads:
silver-lined matte light
Halloween orange, matte
transparent cantaloup, and
transparent gold round

Flared spacers

1. Thread a needle on one end of a 24-in. (61cm) piece of conditioned thread (Basics, p. 104). Create a 16-row ladder (Basics, p. 106), substituting three beads for the single bead in each ladder row **(fig. 1)**. Each row of my ladder consists of a color A bead, a color B, and an A.

2. Create a tube from the ladder by stitching the last row to the first. Sew through the loop again to secure the tube **(fig. 2)**.

3. Pick up two C beads and sew down into the next bead on the ladder. Come up through the next bead and repeat around the tube **(fig. 3)**.

4. To start the next row, come up through the first C bead you added. Pick up two As and sew down into the next C bead. Come up through the next C bead and repeat around the tube **(fig. 4)**.

TIP

If you use unsoldered chain, you can finish the wrapped loops in one step, which may be helpful because keeping the beads and spacers snug is so important. Making organically wrapped loops instead of neat rows will give you some design leeway in case you need to add an extra wrap on one side to tighten things up a bit.

5. Start the herringbone third row by coming up through the first color A bead you added. Pick up two Bs and sew down into the next A bead. Come up through the next A bead and repeat around the tube **(fig. 5)**.

6. Add a fourth finishing row by coming up through the first color B bead you added. Pick up three Cs and sew down into the next B bead and the A underneath it. Come up through the next A and B beads and repeat around the tube **(fig. 6)**. Work the thread through a couple of beads in the diamond. Tie an overhand knot between two beads and trim the excess thread.

7. Thread a needle on one end of an 18-in. (46cm) piece of conditioned thread. Bring the thread up through a color B bead on the other side of the ladder and repeat steps 3–5 **(fig. 7)**. Make a total of four spacers.

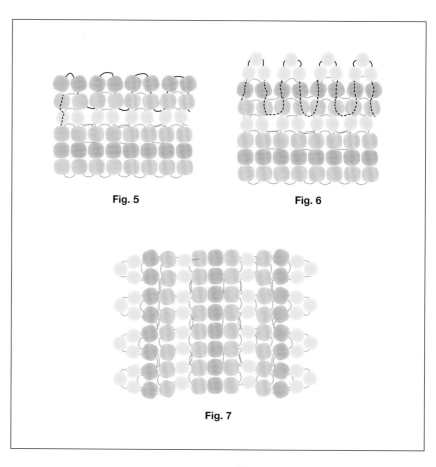

Fig. 5   Fig. 6

Fig. 7

Necklace

1. Cut two 8-in. (20cm) pieces of chain and a 9-in. (23cm) piece of wire. On one end of the wire, make the first half of a wrapped loop (Basics, p. 102), attach a chain, and finish the loops—but don't trim the wire.

2. String an alternating pattern of five pearls and four spacers on the wire. Push the pearls and spacers together so the herringbone is flared against

the beads. Make the first half of a wrapped loop on the end of the wire and attach the other chain. Complete the wraps, making sure the wraps keep the beads snug against the pearls.

3. If you need to, add another wrap to the first loop to keep things taut and even. Then trim the wire on both ends. Attach a jump ring to each end, attaching the lobster-claw clasp with one.

 TIP

I made a monochromatic version of the necklace using pearls I dyed with Rit dye in tangerine.

...minimal = super stylish!

Earrings

For each earring, construct a smaller ladder, add a shorter herringbone fringe, and flair it with a rondelle on each side. Add two accent seed beads on each end of the headpin before making the wrapped loop and attaching the earring wire.

Earrings
- **4** 10mm rondelles
- 1g 11º round seed beads or cylinder beads in three colors
- **48** 15º seed beads
- **2** 3-in. (7.6cm) headpins
- **2** 7mm jump rings
- Pair of earring wires
- Beading thread
- Beading needles, #10–#12
- Scissors
- Thread conditioner

- Roundnose pliers and chainnose pliers
- Diagonal wire cutters

Color Guide
11º cylinder beads: opaque turquoise Delicas
11º round beads: lime green, light azure
15º cylinder beads: metallic gold Delicas

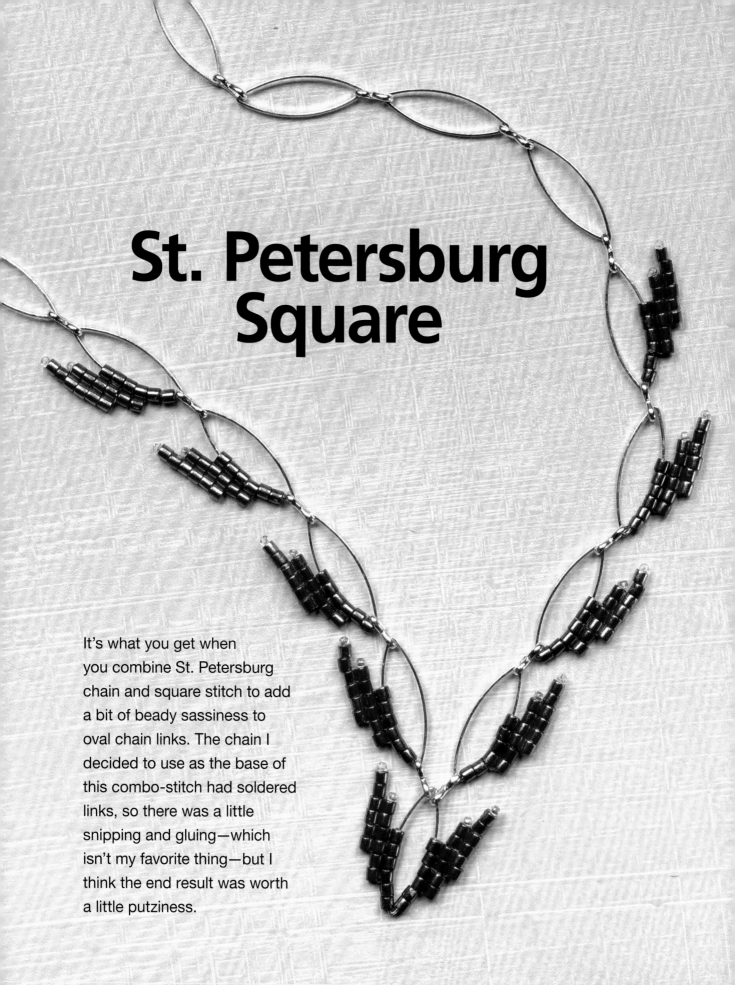

St. Petersburg Square

It's what you get when
you combine St. Petersburg
chain and square stitch to add
a bit of beady sassiness to
oval chain links. The chain I
decided to use as the base of
this combo-stitch had soldered
links, so there was a little
snipping and gluing—which
isn't my favorite thing—but I
think the end result was worth
a little putziness.

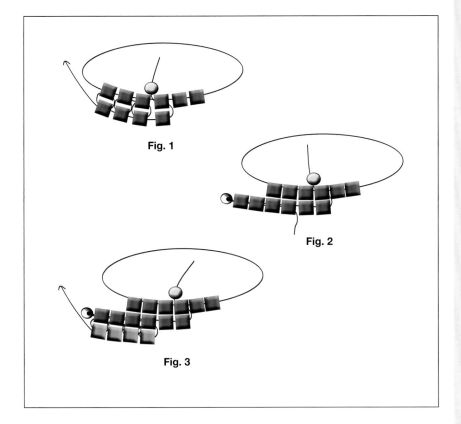

Fig. 1

Fig. 2

Fig. 3

Embellish a side link

1. Use diagonal wire cutters to cut through one side on the chain link about one third the way from the end. Slide six color A 8º cylinder beads onto the cut side. It's not necessary to glue the cut back together, as the 8º will cover the break, but if you want to, this is the time. Use the tiniest bit of glue possible (so you don't obstruct the hole of the 8º bead around it) and let it dry before you begin stitching.

2. Thread a needle at one end of a 12-in. (30cm) piece of conditioned thread. Attach a stop bead (Basics, p. 104). Starting between the fourth and fifth beads from step 1, bring the thread through the fourth bead. Pick up two color B 8º cylinder beads and sew back through the third A and

second B. Pick up a B and sew back through the second A and added B. Pick up a B and sew back through the first A and new B **(fig. 1)**.

3. Pick up two Bs and an 11º round seed bead. Sew back through the two Bs just picked up and the last two Bs added in step 2 **(fig. 2)**.

4. Following step 2, use square stitch to add four color C cylinders to the last four Bs picked up **(fig. 3)**.

Complete step 1 (cutting and gluing) for all links at the same time. By the time you're done, the glue will be dry. As you go along, periodically twirl the beads on the previously glued links to make sure they are not sticking.

Supplies

Large-link necklace, 24 in. (61cm)
- 2g 8º cylinder beads, in each of three colors
- 1g 11º round seed beads
- 24 in. (61cm) 25mm marquise-link chain
- **2** 7mm jump rings
- Lobster-claw clasp

Small-link necklace, 20 in. (50cm)
- 2g 8º cylinder beads, in each of two colors
- 1g 11º seed beads in black
- 20 in. (50cm) 13mm marquise-link chain
- **2** 7mm jump rings
- Lobster claw clasp

Both projects
- Beading thread
- Beading needles, #10–#12
- Scissors
- Thread conditioner
- Roundnose pliers and chainnose pliers
- Diagonal wire cutters
- E6000 and a toothpick

Color Guide
Large-link neckace
8º **cylinder beads:** Duracoat galvanized magenta, Duracoat galvanized dusty orchid, and Duracoat galvanized eggplant Delicas
11º **round seed beads:** transparent silver-lined

Small-link necklace
8º **cylinder beads:** matte metallic dark gray, inside color-lined silver
11º **round seed beads:** transparent silver-lined

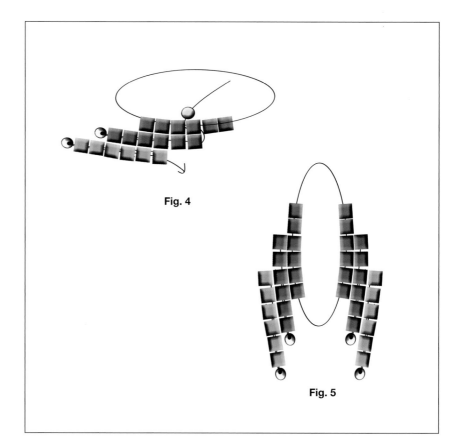

Fig. 4

Fig. 5

The connectors on the large chain were an unexpected help. They allowed me to remove the links to allow the glue to dry while I worked on the others and also covered the cut place on the center link.

5. Pick up two Cs and an 11º. Sew back through the two Cs just picked up and the Cs added in step 4 **(fig. 4)**. Bring the thread back through several beads, tie an overhand knot (Basics, p. 104), and trim the excess thread.

Embellish both sides of a center chain link

1. Use diagonal wire cutters to cut through the link, where the sides meet. Slide six 8º cylinder beads on each side of the link. Apply glue to the break and let it dry.

2. On each side, follow steps 2–5 of embellishing a side link **(fig. 5)**.

Large-link necklace

Find the center link on 24-in. (61cm) length of chain and embellish four links on each side of it, making sure all the embellishments point toward the back of the necklace. Then embellish both sides of the center link. Use a jump ring (Basics, p. 103) to attach a lobster claw clasp on one end of the chain.

When choosing chain for this project, be sure the links are narrow enough for the 8º cylinder beads, but still sturdy enough to maintain shape if you're cutting it. Narrow, unsoldered chain is another option.

...make a mini masterpiece!

Small-link necklace

Skip the center link focal and just orient all the bead segments in the same direction. Shorten each line of beads from six to three for the shorter links.

Earrings

For each earring, separate links of chain and follow the steps for embellishing a side link, but with two-bead rows. Attach the link to an earring wire.

Earrings

- **20** 8º cylinder beads in two colors
- **4** 11º seed beads
- **2** 13mm marquise links of chain
- **2** 7mm jump rings
- Pair of earring wires
- Beading thread
- Beading needles, #10–#12
- Scissors
- Thread conditioner
- Roundnose pliers and chainnose pliers
- Diagonal wire cutters

Color Guide

8º cylinder beads: matte metallic dark gray, inside color-lined silver

11º round seed beads: transparent silver-lined

BASICS

Wirework

Plain loop

1. Using chainnose pliers, make a right-angle bend approximately ¼ in. (6mm) from the end of the wire.
2. Grip the tip of the wire in roundnose pliers. Press downward slightly, and rotate the wire into a loop.

3. Let go, then grip the loop at the same place on the pliers, and keep turning to close the loop. The closer to the tip of the roundnose pliers that you work, the smaller the loop will be.

Wrapped loops

1. Using chainnose pliers, make a right-angle bend approximately 1¼ in. (3.2cm) from the end of the wire. Position the jaws of your roundnose pliers in the bend.
2. Curve the short end of the wire over the top jaw of the roundnose pliers.
3. Reposition the pliers so the lower jaw fits snugly in the loop. Curve the wire downward around the bottom

jaw of the pliers. This is the first half of a wrapped loop.
4. To complete the wraps, grasp the top of the loop with chainnose pliers.
5. Wrap the wire around the stem two or three times. Trim the excess wire, and gently press the cut end close to the wraps with chainnose pliers.

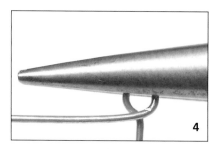

Opening and closing loops or jump rings

1. Hold a loop or jump ring with two pairs of chainnose pliers or with chainnose and bentnose pliers.

2. To open the loop or jump ring, bring the tips of one pair of pliers toward you and push the tips of the other pair away.

3. Reverse the steps to close the loop or jump ring.

Wrapping above a top-drilled bead

1. Center a top-drilled bead on a 3-in. (7.6cm) piece of wire. Bend each wire end upward, crossing them into an X above the bead.

2. Using chainnose pliers, make a small bend in each wire end so they form a right angle.

3. Wrap the horizontal wire around the vertical wire as in a wrapped loop. Trim the excess wrapping wire.

Folded crimp

1. Position the crimp bead in the hole of the crimping pliers that is closest to the handle.

2. Holding the wires apart, squeeze the tool to compress the crimp bead, making sure one wire is on each side of the dent.

3. Place the crimp bead in the front hole of the tool, and position it so the dent is facing outward. Squeeze the tool to fold the crimp in half. Tug on the wires to ensure that the crimp is secure.

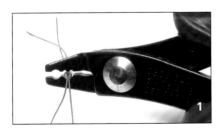 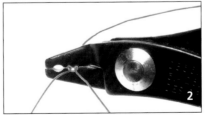 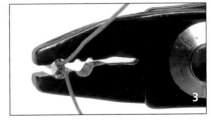

Flat crimp

1. Place the crimp in the jaws of the chainnose pliers.

2. Squeeze the crimp shut.

Knotting

Overhand knot

Make a loop at the end of the thread. Pull the short tail through the loop, and tighten.

Surgeon's knot

Bring the left-hand thread over the right-hand thread twice. Pull the ends to tighten. Cross right over left, and go through the loop. Tighten.

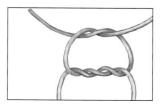

Square knot

1. Bring the left-hand thread over the right-hand thread and around.
2. Cross right over left, and go through the loop.

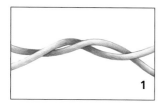 

Half-hitch knot

Exit a bead, and form a loop perpendicular to the thread between beads. Bring the needle under that thread and away from the loop. Then go back over the thread and through the loop. Pull gently so the knot doesn't tighten prematurely.

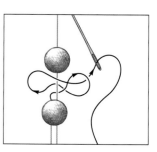

Stitching

Conditioning thread

Use either beeswax (not candle wax or paraffin) or Thread Heaven to condition nylon thread (Nymo). Beeswax smooths the nylon fibers and adds tackiness that will stiffen your beadwork slightly. Thread Heaven adds a static charge that causes the thread to repel itself, so don't use it with doubled thread. Stretch the thread, then pull it through the conditioner, starting with the end that comes off the spool first.

Adding a stop bead

Use a stop bead to secure beads temporarily when you begin stitching. Choose a bead that is distinctly different from the beads in your project. String the stop bead about 6 in. (15cm) from the end of your thread, and go back through it in the same direction. If desired, go through it one more time for added security.

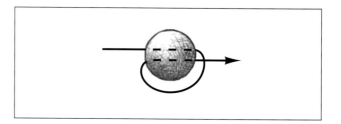

Ending/adding thread

To end a thread, weave back into the beadwork, following the existing thread path and tying two or three half-hitch knots around the thread between beads as you go. Change directions as you weave so the thread crosses itself. Sew through a few beads after the last knot before cutting the thread.

To add a thread, start several rows below the point where the last bead was added, and weave through the beadwork, tying half-hitch knots between beads.

Peyote: flat even-count

1. Pick up an even number of beads **(a–b)**. These beads will shift to form the first two rows.

2. To begin row 3, pick up a bead, skip the last bead strung in the previous step, and sew through the next bead in the opposite direction **(b–c)**. For each stitch, pick up a bead, skip a bead in the previous row, and sew through the next bead, exiting the first bead strung **(c–d)**. The beads added in this row are higher than the previous rows and are referred to as "up-beads."

3. For each stitch in subsequent rows, pick up a bead, and sew through the next up-bead in the previous row **(d–e)**. To count peyote stitch rows, count the total number of beads along both straight edges.

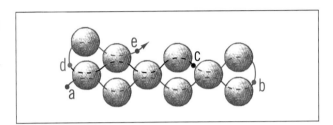

Peyote: flat odd-count

Odd-count peyote is the same as even-count peyote, except for the turn on odd-numbered rows, where the last bead of the row can't be attached in the standard way because there is no up-bead to sew into. The odd-row turn can be convoluted, so we've simplified it here. Please note that the start of this simplified approach is a little different in that the first beads you pick up are the beads in rows 2 and 3. In the next step, you work row 1 and do a simplified turn. After the turn, you'll work the rest of the piece, beginning with row 4.

1. Pick up an odd number of beads. These beads will shift to form rows 2 and 3 in the next step. If you're working a pattern with more than one bead color, make sure you pick up the beads for the correct rows. Work row 3 as in even-count peyote, stopping before adding the last bead.

2. Work a figure-8 turn at the end of row 3: Sew through the first bead picked up in step 1 (bead 1). Pick up the last bead of the row you're working on (bead 8), and sew through beads 2, 3, 7, 2, 1, and 8.

You can work the figure-8 turn at the end of each odd-numbered row, but this will cause this edge to be stiffer than the other. Instead, in subsequent odd-numbered rows, pick up the last bead of the row, sew under the thread bridge between the last two edge beads, and sew back through the last bead added and pick up the next bead to begin the next row.

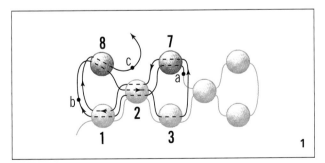

1

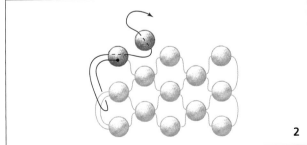

2

Ladder stitch

To work a ladder, pick up two beads, sew through the first bead again, and then sew through the second bead (a–b). Add subsequent beads by picking up one bead, sewing through the previous bead, and then sewing through the new bead (b–c). Continue for the desired length. While this is the most common technique, it produces uneven tension along the ladder of beads because of the alternating pattern of a single thread bridge on the edge between two beads and a double thread bridge on the opposite edge between the same two beads. You can easily correct the uneven tension by zigzagging back through the beads in the opposite direction. Doing this creates a double thread path along both edges of the ladder. This aligns the beads right next to each other but fills the bead holes with extra thread, which can cause a problem if you are using beads with small holes.

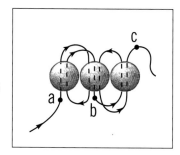

Square stitch

1. String the required number of beads for the first row. Then pick up the first bead of the second row. Go through the last bead of the first row and the first bead of the second row in the same direction as before. The new bead sits on top of the old bead, and the holes are parallel.

2. Pick up the second bead of row 2, and go through the next-to-last bead of row 1. Continue through the new bead of row 2. Repeat this step for the entire row.

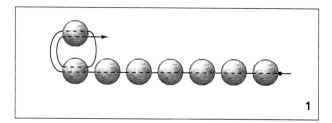

1

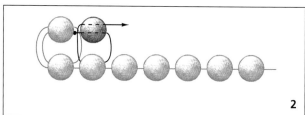

2

Zipping up or joining flat peyote

To join two sections of a flat peyote piece invisibly, match up the two pieces so the edge beads fit together. "Zip up" the pieces by zigzagging through the up-beads on both edges.

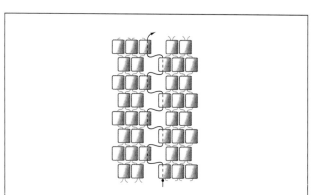

Whipstitch

Whipstitch is a method of hand-sewing seams. Bring the needle through the material on the bottom side of the opening, and push it through the material on the upper side of the opening at an angle as shown. Repeat until the opening has been closed.

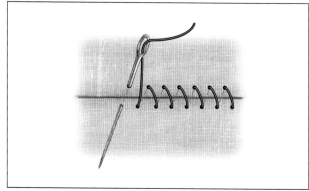

TOOLS AND MATERIALS

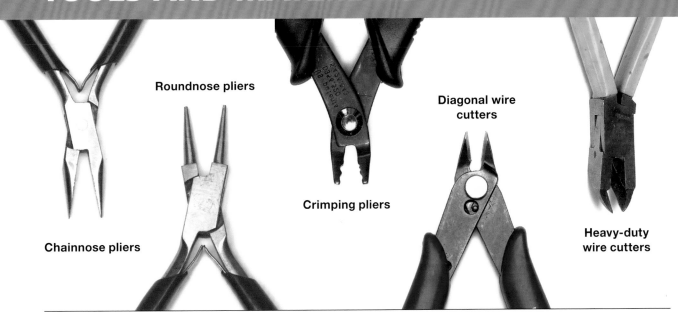

Roundnose pliers

Diagonal wire cutters

Crimping pliers

Heavy-duty wire cutters

Chainnose pliers

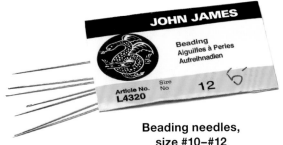

Beading needles, size #10–#12

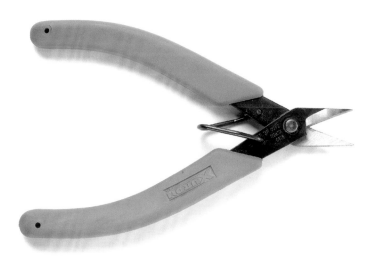

Sharp scissors

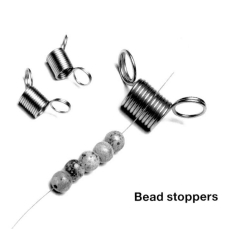

Bead stoppers

Beading wire

Beading thread

Thread conditioner

Wire (silver, gold, copper)

Chain
(various styles)

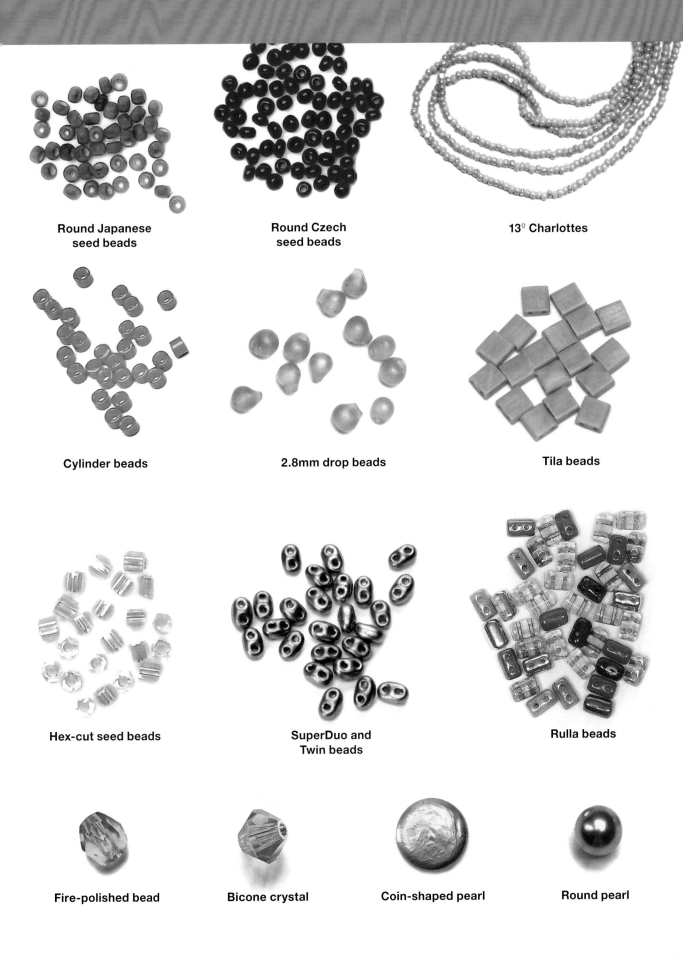

Round Japanese
seed beads

Round Czech
seed beads

13⁰ Charlottes

Cylinder beads

2.8mm drop beads

Tila beads

Hex-cut seed beads

SuperDuo and
Twin beads

Rulla beads

Fire-polished bead

Bicone crystal

Coin-shaped pearl

Round pearl

Clasps: magnetic,
bar, lobster-claw, toggle,
and S-hook

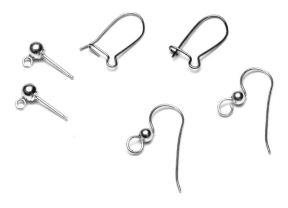

Earring wires:
post, kidney, and
French hook

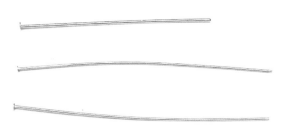

headpins

filigree

Crimp beads and crimp tubes

Jump rings

ABOUT THE AUTHOR

Originally from the Chicago area, Cathy Jakicic moved to Milwaukee to study journalism at Marquette University. She began making jewelry in the wee hours of the morning while working the late shift at Milwaukee's morning newspaper right after college.

She has worked at number of newspapers and magazines since then, including *Bead Style* magazine from 2005 to 2013 where she saw the magazine grow from a spin-off of *Bead&Button* to an industry-leading publication with a vibrant website and a number of digital offerings.

While at *Bead Style*, she wrote two other books on making jewelry: *Hip Handmade Memory Jewelry* and *Jewelry Projects from a Beading Insider.*

Today, she is editing the *"Healthcare Facilities Today"* website for Trade Press Media Group, but still loves exploring all kinds of jewelry making, especially bead weaving, stitching, and embroidery. A long-time supported of Milwaukee's non-profit community, Cathy frequently donates her jewelry to local efforts—primarily those that support the arts as well as the health and welfare of women and families.

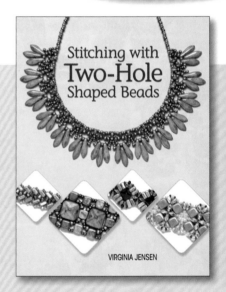

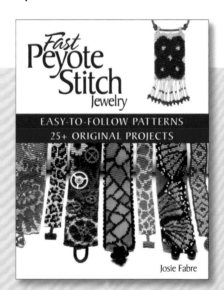